"This project answers the important que
authors and their commitment to makir,
it all close enough to enhance our wisdom, patience, gentleness, and perseverance. The light on the hill will be a bit brighter because of it."

> **Edward T. Welch,** Counselor and Faculty Member, Christian Counseling & Educational Foundation; author, *I Have a Psychiatric Diagnosis: What Does the Bible Say?*

"I believe that this well-written book will help mental health professionals, family members, and those struggling with mental illness. It takes a complex issue and breaks it down into an organized and practical guide of help and healing."

> **Bruce Langerak, DO,** Internal Medicine, Grand Rapids, Michigan

"In an engaging, practical, and insightful commentary, David Murray and Tom Karel Jr. challenge the Christian community to understand and embrace the struggle of mental illness. As a clinician with more than twenty-five years of experience, I am delighted to have this resource at my fingertips. The authors offer a welcome bridge between faith and clinical applications."

> **Emilie DeYoung,** mental health clinician; Clinical Director, Winning at Home, Inc.

"When people and their problems get more complex and acute, two equal and opposite reactions are either to withdraw or to rush in without humility, curiosity, or wisdom. Thankfully, David Murray and Tom Karel Jr. have written a primer for pastors, small-group leaders, family, and everyone in between. I am so thankful for this book and how it has the potential to make the church a safe place for all who struggle and seek to find God's grace in the midst of their suffering. I highly recommend this book!"

> **Tim S. Lane,** President, Institute for Pastoral Care; President, Tim Lane & Associates; author, *How People Change* and *Unstuck*

"There are few topics that have garnered as much interest and discussion in our day as mental health and illness. That is why I'm so grateful for this incredibly helpful resource from David Murray and Tom Karel Jr. They have managed to write a succinct book that is both informative and well-researched but brims with humanity, compassion, and understanding. Whatever role you might play, you will find biblical and practical help from two seasoned individuals who are honest about not only the troubles we face but also the hope we have in Christ. This is a book I know I will return to in my care and counsel of others. I trust the same will be true for you, too."

Jonathan Holmes, Executive Director, Fieldstone Counseling

"*A Christian's Guide to Mental Illness* is the perfect book for those who have questions about how or whether mental illness has any place in their life as a Christian. David Murray and Tom Karel Jr. walk us through questions and concerns some Christians have wrestled with regarding the field of mental health. They provide answers that are clear, practical, personal, and grounded in their deep faith."

Mark Eastburg, CEO, Pine Rest Christian Mental Health Services, Grand Rapids, Michigan

"How does Jesus view mental illness? I suspect this book comes about as close to capturing his understanding and compassion as anything I've read. Bringing together a God-centered approach to life with a deep sensitivity to the needs of Christians with mental illness, it is chock-full of practical wisdom and guidance to help the church become a place where such people feel safe, welcome, and supported—a place where the poor in spirit are being blessed."

Eric L. Johnson, Professor of Christian Psychology, Houston Christian University; author, *God and Soul Care: The Therapeutic Resources of the Christian Faith*

A Christian's Guide to Mental Illness

A Christian's Guide to Mental Illness

Answers to 30 Common Questions

David Murray and Tom Karel Jr.

CROSSWAY®

WHEATON, ILLINOIS

Library of Congress Cataloging-in-Publication Data
Names: Murray, David, 1969- author. | Karel, Thom, Jr., 1969- author.
Title: A Christian's guide to mental illness : answers to 30 common questions / David Murray, Thom Karel Jr.
Description: Wheaton, Illinois : Crossway, [2023]. | Includes bibliographical references and index.
Identifiers: LCCN 2022054289 (print) | LCCN 2022054290 (ebook) | ISBN 9781433587276 (trade paperback) | ISBN 9781433587283 (pdf) | ISBN 9781433587306 (epub)
Subjects: LCSH: Mental illness—Religious aspects—Christianity—Miscellanea. | Christianity—Psychology—Miscellanea. | Psychiatry and religion—Miscellanea.
Classification: LCC BT732.4 .M87 2023 (print) | LCC BT732.4 (ebook) | DDC 261.8/322—dc23/eng/20230417
LC record available at https://lccn.loc.gov/2022054289
LC ebook record available at https://lccn.loc.gov/2022054290

Crossway is a publishing ministry of Good News Publishers.

VP										
		32	31	30	29	28	27	26	25	24	23
15	14	13	12	11	10	9	8	7	6	5	4	3	2	1

David
To Ed Stetzer, whose Christlike compassion for sufferers has shaped
me, and whose research expertise has shaped this book.

Tom
To my dear wife Ruthanne and our precious daughters
Hannah, Gabby, and Lydia: your encouragement and
prayers have helped me every step of the way.

Contents

Introduction

WHAT DO YOU THINK when you hear one of these words: "depression," "anxiety," "bipolar disorder," "schizophrenia," "eating disorder," "obsessive compulsive disorder (OCD)," and so on? You probably try not to think about them, and hope you never have to. But, with one in five American adults suffering mental illness at some point in their lives, sooner or later someone we love in our family, among our friends, or at church will bring one of these scary labels to life in our lives.[1]

As anyone who has gone through this knows, when one person suffers with a mental illness, it sends tumultuous waves into multiple lives. Spouses, parents, siblings, friends, pastors, elders, neighbors

---

1 In 2019, about 1 in 10 American adults reported symptoms of anxiety or depressive disorder. In 2020, it rose to 4 in 10, a fourfold increase (Nirmita Panchal, et al., "The Implications of COVID-19 for Mental Health and Substance Use," Kaiser Family Foundation, https://www .kff.org/coronavirus-covid-19/issue-brief/the-implications-of-covid-19-for-mental-health -and-substance-use/). Lockdowns, social isolation, cancelation of sports and graduations, and educational disruptions have had a particularly devastating effect on teens and children. Forty-six percent of parents report new or worsening mental health in their teens during 2020, with 1 in 3 girls and 1 in 5 boys reporting new or worsening anxiety (National Poll on Children's Health, https://mottpoll.org/reports/how-pandemic-has-impacted-teen-mental -health). Some recent studies have found more than 50 percent of children suffering mild to severe depression, anxiety, or insomnia.

are called into demanding roles and responsibilities that they are not prepared for, frequently leading to a sense of helplessness and hopelessness. "How can I help? Where can I get help? Who else can help? Is there any help that will help?"

We know how people react in these situations because not only have we been involved in counseling for decades, we've both been surprised by depression and anxiety in our own lives. Yes, the counselors needed counseling!

Through all this, we've identified the most common questions asked by sufferers, their families, friends, and churches (the thirty questions we ask in this handbook). But we've also learned and lived answers to these questions through practicing a holistic Christian approach to mental illness. The answers are designed to be as simple and practical as possible so that family, friends, and churches can work together to help those who suffer with mental illness, giving them and us hope. Before we find that hope and help, let's first identify the causes of the hopelessness and helplessness we experience when mental illness strikes someone we love.

We Are Hopeless and Helpless

We suffer from despair and defeatism because mental illness is hard to understand. Apart from a few rare exceptions, there is no test to confirm the existence of mental illness, tell us what's gone wrong, or show us how to put it right. While we will discuss a range of causes in these pages, it's often impossible to know which one or which combination of causes were relevant in each case. There's a mystery in it at times, which science has never fully understood or explained.

Despondency and discouragement also set in for us when sufferers refuse to even admit there is a problem, are pessimistic about their chances of recovery, or refuse to accept offered help. This denial or defeatism makes it especially difficult for family, friends, pastors, counselors, or doctors who want to help them.

But the most horrendous hopelessness and helplessness can sink us when we see the way that mental illness damages a Christian's faith and witness. We look on with horror as we see someone we thought was a Christian in a state of deep despair, dark depression, or fearful anxiety. Sometimes it shatters a Christian's faith, so that he has no sense of God, or worse, a sense that God has forsaken him or turned against him. In extreme cases, some may even think that *they* are God. How can someone be a Christian when he is characterized by hearing voices, bizarre behavior, chaotic unpredictability, detachment from reality, or shameful sin? There don't appear to be any fruits of the Spirit, but only works of the flesh (Gal. 5:19–23), raising huge questions such as, "Can someone who is a Christian feel like that? Think like that? Act like that?"

The spiritual torture of those questions for the loved ones of the mentally ill is part of the motivation behind this book. Norman and Vicki Van Mersbergen approached us a few years ago with a small legacy from the estate of Norman's brother Gary, who passed away following complications related to schizophrenia. Although Gary had professed faith early in life, that was soon followed by three decades of mental instability.[2]

This painful personal experience of mental illness prompted many questions for Norman and Vicki: What comfort can we give loved ones amid such struggles? Are there any ways we can discern the fruits of the Spirit in a mentally ill person? If so, how do we do so and how do we minister to sufferers? What can the church do better, both for the mentally ill and for those who care for them?

---

2 You can read their story at the conclusion of this book.

Together, we decided to use Gary's legacy to fund research into these and similar questions, and we are most grateful for our research partners, Lifeway Research and Focus on the Family, and their published findings.[3] Norman and Vicki's desire to share the results of our research with a wider audience and to turn it into a practical Christian guide for friends and family of the mentally ill resulted in this book. So where do we get hope and help amid hopelessness and helplessness?

God Gives Hope and Help

As the authors of this book, we want to assure readers that God is our hope and help. For a combined total of about fifty years, we've both been involved in helping Christians with mental illness and their families. Tom has served as a psychologist in a Christian healthcare setting and David has served as a pastor, counselor, and professor of counseling, as well as authoring various books on the subject.[4]

---

3 Lifeway interviewed 1,000 pastors, 355 adults diagnosed with acute mental illness, 207 family members of the mentally ill, and 15 mental health professionals. They covered topics such as the experience of mental illness, its impact on life (especially spiritual life), and the role of caring professions, churches, pastors, and mental health professionals. This work resulted in two reports, *Study of Acute Mental Illness and Christian Faith*, published by Lifeway Research (September 2014), https://research.lifeway.com/wp-content/uploads/2014/09/Acute-Mental -Illness-and-Christian-Faith-Research-Report-1.pdf; and *Serving Those with Mental Illness*, published by Focus on the Family (September 2014), https://media.focusonthefamily.com /pastoral/pdf/PAS_eBook_Series_Mental_Health_INTERACTIVE.pdf; and one theological paper, *Salvation and the Mentally Ill: Can Someone Who Lacks Mental Abilities Spend Eternity with God?* (Nashville: Lifeway, unpublished).

4 E.g., David Murray, *Christians Get Depressed Too: Hope and Help for Depressed People* (Grand Rapids, MI: Reformation Heritage, 2010); *The Happy Christian: Ten Ways to Be a Joyful Believer in a Gloomy World* (Nashville: Thomas Nelson, 2015); *Reset: Living a Grace-Paced Life in a Burnout Culture* (Wheaton, IL: Crossway, 2017); *Why Am I Feeling Like This? A Teen's Guide to Freedom from Anxiety and Depression* (Wheaton, IL: Crossway, 2020); *Why Is My Teenager Feeling Like This? A Guide for Helping Teens through Anxiety and Depression*

Most importantly, we have both suffered with bouts of depression and anxiety in recent times. Although these painful times delayed this book for a few years, we believe it was God's delay and has resulted in a better book as well as a better us. When caregivers become care-receivers, it makes them better caregivers.

We approach this problem as Christians who not only believe but who have experienced that God provides hope and help for Christians with mental illness and those who care for them. While mental illness often has spiritual consequences, it is rarely only a spiritual problem that can be fixed simply with repentance and faith. God provides hope and help through his word and a word-based view of his world. This word-directed, holistic approach is the most honoring to God and the most beneficial for sufferers and their families.

As noted, this handbook is organized around thirty questions and answers that we've found are those most commonly asked by perplexed parents, spouses, friends, and pastors. We've tried to be ruthlessly practical, discussing only enough theory to help readers understand and have confidence in the practical directions, and grounding it all in biblical truth. We suggest you do a quick read of the whole book to get a big-picture view of how to help sufferers, then return to a closer study of chapters especially relevant to you, and then keep the book handy for reference purposes and answers to future questions. We also encourage church leaders to use this book to develop a holistic approach to caring for those with mental illness in their church and community.

There is no quick fix for mental illness. However, with faith in the Helper of the helpless and the Hope of the hopeless, all Christians can offer Christlike care to the mentally ill, giving help and hope to the helpless and hopeless.

(Wheaton, IL: Crossway, 2020); Shona Murray and David Murray, *Refresh: Embracing a Grace-Paced Life in a World of Endless Demands* (Wheaton, IL: Crossway, 2017).

1

What Is Mental Illness?

BEFORE YOU READ ANY FURTHER, think about the question posed by this chapter's title and try to answer it.

It's challenging, isn't it?

Maybe you answered, "It's a sin," or, "It's a weakness," or, "It's a sickness," or perhaps even, "It's not real," or, "I don't like that term." But most likely, you said something like, "I'm not sure," or, "To be honest, I really have no idea."

Despite improved research and education, many of us are still confused, uncertain, or simply wrong about what we think mental illness is. Consequently, we shy away from the topic. Some blame and condemn those who suffer with it. Others, usually unintentionally, harm rather than help. The absence of sympathy and lack of understanding add additional layers of suffering to the problem, compounding the hurt and deterring people from seeking help.

This book will give you a better handle on mental illness and guide you toward more loving responses—emotionally, verbally, and practically. Our aim is to replace confusion, error, and misunderstanding with clarity, truth, and education so that we all can be more effective in caring for the mentally ill.[1] In the next chapter, we'll discuss the pros and cons of using the term "mental illness." For now, as we begin to answer the question, What is mental illness?, we need to understand four foundational aspects of it.

Mental Illness Is an Old Problem

Mental illness was not part of the original creation. When God made everything, including the first man and woman, he pronounced everything "very good" (Gen. 1:31). Humanity was perfect in every way: physically, mentally, emotionally, relationally, vocationally, and spiritually.

Once sin entered the world through Adam and Eve's choices, all humanity came under the divine curse together with the rest of the creation (Gen. 3:14–19). Every part of us became disordered and broken, including our bodies, minds, emotions, and souls (Rom. 8:20–22). Illness, including mental illness, was now a part of humanity. All depression, anxiety, bipolar disorder, schizophrenia, PTSD, personality disorders, and so forth, can be traced to this terrible turning point in world history. That's how long mental illness has been around. It's an old problem.

Some Christians believe that mental illness is simply a modern idea dreamed up by God-defying psychiatrists, soul-denying psychologists, money-making drug companies, and blame-shifting sinners. Church history says otherwise (as does modern medical research). To give just one example, mental illness was accepted

1 Lifeway's interviews with mental health experts found that "education is the most needed resource." Specifically, "individuals, families, churches, and pastors all need clarity on (1) the basics of mental illness; (2) signs of what to look for; (3) knowing how to respond if they suspect someone has a mental illness; (4) ways to be supportive without being overwhelmed" (Lifeway Research, *Study of Acute Mental Illness and Christian Faith*, 5, https://research.lifeway.com/wp-content/uploads /2014/09/Acute-Mental-Illness-and-Christian-Faith-Research-Report-1.pdf).

8

as genuine and treated seriously by some of the greatest Christian experts in soul care that God has ever given to his church—the Puritans. In days of spiritual revival and reformation, these spiritual giants and geniuses had deep insights into the causes and cures of mental illness that we would do well to learn from today.[2] Understanding this historical background together with some modern research on the brain (especially the physical changes that may occur) should help reduce the amount of shame and social stigma around mental illness.[3]

When sin invaded the world,
mental illness invaded our minds.

If mental illness has been around for so long, though, how come there's still so little understanding of it or agreement about what it is? One reason is that it's such a complex problem.

Mental Illness Is a Complex Problem

Some mental illness can have a relatively simple fix, but usually it's a lot more complicated. That is because it affects, and is affected by, multiple parts of our humanity. A broken arm affects only a small part of our body, impacts only a couple of areas of our lives, and needs only one or two visits to the doctor. Other illnesses, like

---

2   See, for example, Richard Baxter's *Preservatives against Melancholy and Over-Much Sorrow* (Charleston, SC: BiblioLife, Gale ECCO Print Editions, 2018), in which he carefully distinguishes spiritual depression (which is cured by faith) from physical depression (which is cured by medicine). In fact he has a whole section on "Medical Care for Those with Depression."

3   Lifeway Research, *Acute Mental Illness and Christian Faith*, 4.

cancer, can affect the entire body and every part of our lives and require lots of professional help.

Mental illness is like cancer in that respect. To one degree or another, nothing can escape its reach. It especially disturbs our thoughts, feelings, and souls, which in turn worsens the mental illness and makes it extremely difficult to figure out what the problem is and what the solutions are. It often requires multiple appointments with various professionals to obtain the necessary help. It's a complex problem that defies simplification.

Over-simplifying mental illness
underestimates mental illness.

"But, if it's so complex, what should we expect in the lives of sufferers?"

We can expect a lot of complexity in the wide range of people who battle mental illness and in their wide-ranging experiences.

Mental Illness Is a Varied Problem

Mental illness is varied in terms of who suffers with it. Although there are some caricatures of who can become mentally ill, there is no one kind of person or personality that is more susceptible. Men and women, old and young, black and white, Type A and Type Z, successful and unsuccessful, believers and unbelievers, and so on; all kinds and types can suffer in this way. It can affect everyone and anyone. Although some families may have a greater risk of being affected due to genetics, no family is immune.

We will see the variety even more clearly in chapter 3 when we look at the different kinds of mental illness, and how statistically common it is. According to one source, in the course of a normal year, almost 1-in-5 American adults will experience a diagnosable mental health disorder, and that rises to 46 percent over the course of a lifetime.[4]

Mental illness is also varied in terms of the nature and severity of symptoms. Each category of mental illness has a range of symptoms associated with it, but what a person actually experiences is greatly influenced by their circumstances. This means that some are slightly impaired in their functioning, others are paralyzed, and most move backward and forward along this scale.

The timing and duration of any given symptom or onset is diverse as well. It can begin when everything is going well, or when everything is going terribly, or even many years after traumatic events. It can last for weeks, months, years, and can even be lifelong. Mental illness can be a one-off episode or something that is repeated. It's a varied problem that defies stereotypes.

If we stereotype mental illness,
we'll overlook mental illness.

"If it's so complex and so varied, is there really anything that can be done to treat it?"

Yes, and it should be treated urgently.

---

4 "The National Survey on Drug Use and Health," *Substance Abuse and Mental Health Administration*, September 2014, http://www.samhsa.gov/data/sites/default/files/sr170-mental-illness-state-estimates-2014/sr170-mental-illness-state-estimates-2014/sr170-mental-illness-state-estimates-2014.htm.

Mental Illness Is an Urgent Problem

Although mental illness can be mild, it usually has serious, life-altering impacts. Many illnesses and problems impede portions of our lives, but mental illness tends to damage every aspect of our lives. It isn't something that can be boxed up and limited easily. Unfortunately, and sadly, because of the far-reaching ripple effects, it can damage our marriages, our children, our careers, our bodies, and our souls. At its most devastating, it deceives people into wanting to end their life.

This is not something to be ignored. Mental illness rarely resolves itself. The deeper we sink into the pit, the harder it is to climb out of it. The longer it is ignored, the worse the consequences. Later in this book, we will look at some of the serious physical consequences of mental illness—the damage to our brains, bones, and other parts of our bodies if left untreated. It is an urgent problem that should be addressed today, not tomorrow.

---

*Mental illness is a today problem,
not a tomorrow problem.*

SUMMARY

Problem: The ignorance, error, and confusion surrounding mental illness reduces our sympathy, desire, and ability to help, which only inflicts more harm on those who are suffering.

Insights: Mental illness is (1) an old problem, (2) a complex problem, (3) a varied problem, and (4) an urgent problem.

Action: Let's educate ourselves about what mental illness is, so that we will respond to it more sympathetically and helpfully.

- Ask God to replace your prejudices, error, and confusion with truth, facts, and clarity.
- Listen to the stories of those with mental illness or read books they have written.
- Read medical research that is often published in simplified form in the media.
- Encourage sufferers to seek help speedily.

David's Story

I cannot remember anyone talking about mental illness when I was growing up in the '70s and '80s. I do remember a popular teen girl in the grade above me committing suicide, but no one talked about it. I grew up in churches, schools, and a family that never discussed mental illness. I went to seminary in my mid-twenties, but it was barely mentioned there. Not surprisingly, my ignorance resulted in a lot of prejudice and error. What made that worse was that I took these mistaken views into my first years of ministry. I so much wish that this simple question, "What is mental illness?," had been addressed at least once in my education. It would have profoundly impacted my ministry. I would have loved better, served better, and at the end of the day I would have been more useful and less harmful.

It may also have prevented (or shortened) my own bout of mental illness. As we continue to explore answers to this question, I hope this book will do for you what I wish had been done for me.

2

Is "Mental Illness" a Helpful Label?

LABELS CAN BE HELPFUL in beginning to describe or define what we are talking about. For example, when we label something as "a sports car," that gives us all an idea, a mental image, of what we're discussing. Without going into lots of detail, it conveniently distinguishes it from, say, a minivan.

However, labels can also cause difficulties. When some people hear the label "sports car," they may think of a classic open-top Corvette. Others may think of a Ferrari Testarossa. Labels can cause miscommunication and misunderstanding because they deal with generalities, not details.

That's why considerable controversy has arisen over the label "mental illness" and whether or when such a label should be used. There's no doubt that "mental illness" has become one of the most overused diagnoses today. It now covers everything from schizophrenia to alcoholism and even pedophilia. It is frequently used to minimize responsibility and to blame all events and actions on factors beyond our control.

This overuse, in turn, has led some to *underuse* the label. If people are misusing it to excuse sin or evade accountability, then it's a term we must avoid, they argue. Others even deny there is any such thing as mental illness, attributing everything to people's wrong choices. The term has also been abused, especially in the media and in movies, to portray people as crazed lunatics or even demonic. Little wonder that many people are scared of this label or hesitant to use it.

Given its difficulties and complications, we must ask if there is any benefit in retaining the term "mental illness," and, if so, how do we use it helpfully? Let's navigate our way through the pros and cons of this label so that we can use the right label in the right way. We'll begin by building awareness of its limitations.

The Label Has Limits

Part of the difficulty that leads to both overuse and underuse of this label is the ambiguity in both of the words, "mental" and "illness."

For example, "mental" suggests it's just something to do with our thoughts, and therefore something exclusively to do with our brains. It can be, but it's often experienced primarily in the emotions (e.g., sadness, anger, fear) rather than in our thoughts. Also, "mental" tends to distance the problem from any spiritual or "heart" component and therefore diminishes or even excludes pastoral and spiritual input. It also fails to account for situational or social factors.

"Illness" is helpful in that it points to a physical or biological problem requiring medical help. The National Alliance on Mental Illness (NAMI) defines mental illnesses as, "medical conditions that disrupt a person's thinking, feeling, mood, ability to relate to others and daily functioning" and "often result in a diminished capacity for coping with the ordinary demands of life."[1]

---

1   *About Mental Illness*, NAMI California, https://namica.org/what-is-mental-illness/.

It can be this, but, unlike many medical conditions, mental illness can rarely be identified with medical tests and is rarely cured with medical input alone. "Illness" implies that it's something just like diabetes or epilepsy, a disease or disorder that always just happens to us, that we have no control over, and that therefore we are not responsible for. This tends to turn the sufferer into a passive victim rather than someone with some responsibilities.

The term "mental illness" is also excessively broad, just like the label "sports car." It gives us a broad, general idea of what we're talking about, but it fails to give us any details. It's like saying someone has an "orthopedic problem" without specifying whether it is a broken toe or a broken neck. "Mental illness" can be incapacitating for years, and can even lead to suicide, or it can be something that people get treatment for while continuing to function at a very high level.

The term "mental illness" has limitations because its range has few limits.

So, if the label has such serious limitations, should we use it at all?

The Label Can Be a Helpful Starting Point

Despite its limitations, "mental illness" is still the preferred label in the medical profession and in popular culture. Although it creates difficulties, it does direct us to a general category that distinguishes it from other issues. Just as the term "orthopedic problem" distinguishes it from "kidney problem" or "heart problem," so "mental illness" serves a similar function.

As such, it can be a helpful starting point, a way of orienting ourselves to what area we are talking about. For example, if friends suggest a trip to Europe this summer, you will have a general idea of what kind of vacation they are proposing. You will know which part of the map to look at (i.e., not Africa or Australia), but you will then want to get a lot more detail about which country, which parts of which country, what activities are planned, and so on.

Just as we would be foolish to agree to a trip to Europe without asking lots of questions about the details, so it is unwise to use the label "mental illness" without asking many more questions. But it's still a useful start-point, if we remain aware of its limitations and go on to ask for more details.

While offering compassionate help to those who suffer due to having fallen bodies and brains, or because of factors outside of their control (see Job 1), or because of direct divine intervention (John 9:3), we must also carefully identify where people have brought some of their suffering upon themselves due to sinful personal choices, and adjust our language, counsel, and help accordingly.

Having weighed the pros and cons, we've reluctantly decided to retain the use of the label "mental illness" in this book. But, when we use the term, we want you to know that we are not minimizing the spiritual component or the sufferer's responsibility, nor are we denying that the suffering is frequently more in the feelings than in the thoughts. Although we will often use the word "sufferer" because we want to communicate sympathy, we are not doing so to deny the involvement of personal sin in some cases or the need for the person to take some responsibility.

"Mental illness" is not a final destination
but a discussion starter.

So, should we use this label in everyday life? Here's one change we can make right away.

The Label Applies to a Problem, Not a Person

Just as it is no longer acceptable to say, "She's disabled," but rather, "She has a disability," so we should avoid saying, "he is mentally ill," or "I am mentally ill." Rather, we should say, "He has a mental illness," or "I have a mental illness."

This important switch applies the label to the problem, not the person, and therefore defines the problem the person has, rather than defining the person as a problem. The switch of verb from "is" to "has" ensures that a person is not defined in their entirety by their problem. A person is much more than an illness, and recovery is not advanced if we inadvertently imply otherwise. It doesn't help the sufferer, and it doesn't help us. A person is much more than their diagnosis, even if their suffering impacts their whole life.

"Mental illness" defines the problem,
not the person.

SUMMARY

Problem: The label "mental illness" is controversial and problematic due to overuse, underuse, and abuse.

Insights: The label "mental illness" (1) has limits, (2) can be a helpful starting point, (3) applies to a problem, not a person.

Action: Recognize the uses and limits of the label "mental illness" and use it wisely, especially when attaching it to a person.

- Discuss the label "mental illness" with someone who is suffering with it. Ask them what they understand by the term, what they find helpful or unhelpful about it.
- Consider the pros and cons of some of the alternative labels: mental disorder, emotional disorder, brain malfunction, broken mind, mental health condition, and so forth.
- How might we help sufferers avoid defining themselves by their mental illness?

Tom's Story

In my clinical practice and in my personal life, I have talked with people suffering with anxiety, depression, or some other mental health diagnosis who have told me, "I am depressed," or "I am bipolar." So often in the struggle with a mental illness, people begin to so identify with the diagnosis that they begin to believe that this defines who they are as a person. In other words, the illness somehow becomes their identity.

Many seem rather surprised at my reaction to this: "You have an illness, an affliction that is a heavy burden to bear. However, this does not define you."

We do not want to err in downplaying the reality of illness of any kind, but neither do we want to err in believing that an illness has the power to overshadow the unique combination of God-given talents, gifts, experiences, and personality that make up a human being created in the image of God.

3

What Are the Different Kinds of Mental Illness?

ONE DISADVANTAGE OF THE LABEL "mental illness" is that it's a broad and general term. It doesn't give much information as to the specific symptoms or the severity and scope of impairment. When people use it, they are usually identifying something abnormal or unstable in how someone thinks or feels, which leads to problems in how they view themselves and the world, and in how they act.

We must go beyond the general term "mental illness" to really understand what the problem is and how to help. To do this, we need to define the nature of the malfunction and the level of impairment. By asking the right questions and listening for the answers, we can get a better understanding of what's wrong and how to minister to sufferers.

If we don't take this further step to accurately define the problem, we may end up with confusion, or even wrong or harmful solutions. A mental illness may end up being treated as a bigger issue than it really is, or being taken less seriously than it should be.

We can begin to address these potential pitfalls by identifying the two main types of mental illness (although there is often overlap, and both may be present in one person). The two categories are primarily affective (mood) disorders, and primarily thought (mind) disorders. Let's look at these categories and what they cover so that we can understand mental illness better and therefore be better able to help.[1]

Primarily Mood (Affective) Disorders

Affective disorders primarily affect the mood or emotions and include anxiety, depression, and bipolar disorder. But even these are general or umbrella terms under which are many different diagnoses or subcategories.

Anxiety

Everyone experiences some measure of anxiety from time to time. It becomes a disorder when it does not go away, it gets worse, or it interferes with normal functioning. About 19 percent of US adults experience an anxiety disorder in any one year, and 31 percent of US adults experience an anxiety disorder in their lifetime.[2] These disorders share certain features but also differ, depending on the objects or situations that provoke them. The main anxiety disorders are:

- *Generalized anxiety disorder.* Excessive anxiety or worry about everyday life, experienced most days for at least six months.
- *Social anxiety disorder.* Paralyzing fear about social evaluation or performance level.

---

1   For more detailed definitions of each disorder, see Lifeway Research, *Study of Acute Mental Illness and Christian Faith*, 3, https://research.lifeway.com/wp-content/uploads/2014/09/Acute-Mental-Illness-and-Christian-Faith-Research-Report-1.pdf.
2   "Any Anxiety Disorder," *National Institute of Mental Health*, https://www.nimh.nih.gov/health/statistics/any-anxiety-disorder.shtml.

- *Obsessive compulsive disorder (OCD).* Long-term uncontrollable thoughts and behaviors that are repeated over and over.
- *Post-traumatic stress disorder.* Anxiety that occurs after the experience of a traumatic event, often manifested in mental and emotional reliving of the event, sometimes in response to "trigger" situations.
- *Panic disorder.* Repeated, intense, temporary, and often unexpected experiences of overwhelming fear.
- *Specific phobia.* Intense and disproportionate fear of a specific object or situation (e.g., fear of flying, open spaces, heights).

Somebody with an anxiety disorder becomes unreasonably fearful in specific situations or in life in general. They may feel restless, jumpy, or out of control. They often have obsessive and repetitive thoughts that focus on their fear. This, in turn, leads to bodily symptoms such as a racing heart, elevated blood pressure, sweating, shortness of breath, and difficulty sleeping. The degree to which and the circumstances in which this is experienced will tend to drive the diagnosis and treatment that is prescribed.

Depression

As with anxiety, everyone becomes sad at some points in life, but depression interferes with life and often incapacitates people. Seven to 8 percent of adults in the US deal with depression each year.[3] This includes the following subcategories:

---

3 "Depression Statistics," Depression and Bipolar Support Alliance, https://www.dbsalliance .org/education/depression/statistics/.

- *Persistent depressive disorder (dysthymia).* Long-term (over two years), low-grade depression, with some major depressive episodes.
- *Major depressive disorder (clinical depression).* Continuous and intense feelings of sadness for long periods of time, the major cause of disability in the US for ages 15–44.
- *Reactive (or situational) depression.* Triggered by difficult life events or experiences (e.g., bereavement, loss of job).
- *Post-partum depression.* This goes beyond normal "baby blues," lasts much longer, and is characterized by extreme sadness, exhaustion, anxiety, and incapacity. It affects about 10–15 percent of US women.

In depression, there is not only a sadness or depressed mood but also a persistent gloominess about the future. The person usually feels a sense of hopelessness or worthlessness. It often includes fatigue, low energy and motivation, a desire to sleep most of the time (and in many cases an inability to get good, refreshing, restful sleep). In severe cases, there may also be a despairing of life to the extent that the person considers or plans for their own death. This is why some refer to depression as a potentially fatal illness.

Bipolar Disorder

The term "bipolar" is now used instead of "manic depression," although they refer to the same disorder. The term describes someone who experiences the two (bi) ends (poles) of the mood spectrum (high and low) in a short period of time. It affects about 3 percent of the US population each year.[4]

---

4 "Depression: Facts, Statistics, and You," *Healthline*, https://www.healthline.com/health/depression/facts-statistics-infographic#2.

Someone with a bipolar disorder may have episodes of debilitating depression. However, several days or weeks later, they may be so full of energy, creativity, and impulsivity that they are unable to sleep or to slow down physically or cognitively (racing thoughts). During these times, their speech and behavior speeds up, and they often get impatient with others who cannot seem to keep up with their racing thoughts or understand their impulsive (and sometimes reckless) behavior.[5]

A mood disorder
is not merely moodiness.

When you learn about these three main categories of affective disorder, you may respond, "But I thought mental illness was mainly mental?" Well, there are some types that are.

Primarily Mind (Thought) Disorders

While the affective disorders are often disabling and devastating, perhaps more confusing and perplexing are the diagnoses classified under "thought disorders." These diagnoses would include:

- *Schizophrenia.* Usually severe disabling thoughts and emotions that result in serious disruption of a person's life.
- *Psychosis.* Contact is lost with external reality, resulting in delusions (false fixed beliefs) and hallucinations (seeing, hearing, smelling what is nonexistent). It often goes along with severe depression.

5 "Bipolar frequently causes a great deal of strain on the patient's closest relationships" (Lifeway Research, *Acute Mental Illness and Christian Faith*, 3).

When a person suffers from one of these disorders, there is a persistent struggle to think and to perceive the world accurately, to make sense out of reality. For instance, a person with a diagnosis of paranoid schizophrenia (one of a number of types of schizophrenia) may be very fearful of things that are not real. Some of the most typical beliefs are:

- I'm being watched or spied on.
- People are trying to kill me.
- People are reading my thoughts.
- I have a special mission from God (or the president).
- I'm hearing voices in my head.
- I can see things other people cannot see (e.g., imaginary friends or enemies).

The person may have some awareness of the unreality of this but may be rather reluctant to reveal what they are thinking for fear of being thought to be "crazy."

In both mood and mind disorders, we also want to ask further questions about the nature and degree of the symptoms and condition in order to gauge severity:

- Is it the first episode or a recurrent one?
- Is it transient/acute (likely to resolve in a relatively short amount of time)?
- Is it persistent/chronic (multiple episodes, waxes and wanes over time)?
- What's the level of impairment (how much does it impact the person's daily functioning)?

When a mind is disordered to any degree,
a life is disordered to some degree.

So, mental illness can be manifested in the mood and in the mind, in feelings and thoughts. And it can vary in frequency, degree, length, and impact. Hopefully this further step in identifying and measuring mental illness will result in better responses to it.

SUMMARY

Problem: Misidentifying mental illness results in confusion, overreaction, underreaction, or wrong solutions.

Insights: There are two main types of mental illness: (1) mood disorders and (2) mind disorders, both of which can vary in degree, length, and impact.

Action: Be able to identify the two main types of mental illness, and some of the main subtypes.

- Talk to mental health professionals and ask them to explain their own experience in dealing with these disorders.
- In what ways have you misunderstood mental illness in the past, and how has that affected others?
- Think of people who may have these disorders. How will you change the way you deal with them and try to help them?

Tom's Story about Scott

Scott, a twenty-one-year-old college student, was brought into my office by his father. Although Scott made clear that he did not want to be there, he did concede that life had not been going well over the past year. Previously an outgoing young man and a straight-A student, he was now withdrawn from family and friends and had failing grades. He was living with his parents, avoiding contact with anyone, and refusing to talk to his parents, siblings, friends, and youth pastor (all of whom he had been close to in the past).

Initially he was perceived as rebellious and possibly back-slidden in his walk with God. However, a family friend and medical doctor recommended Scott and his parents talk with me. The initial sessions focused on listening to Scott and his family describe the symptoms and events that had brought them there. Scott admitted that he had become more recluse due to becoming very fearful (paranoid) and hearing voices; this guided us to a general diagnosis of mental illness. Using clarifying questions similar to those in this chapter, I was able to identify the specific mental illness of paranoid schizophrenia, and an appropriate treatment plan was soon under way. Scott's family and church family were committed to supporting him through treatment, to educating themselves on Scott's mental illness diagnosis, and to assisting him in reintegrating back into family and church life.

4

How Is Mental Illness Different from Ordinary Sadness, Anxiety, and Confusion?

MENTAL AND EMOTIONAL DISTRESS is a normal part of living in an abnormal world. Because of our fallen and sinful world, we can all expect to be sad, anxious, or confused from time to time. So how do we distinguish "normal abnormality" from abnormal abnormality? Or, to put it another way, at what point does sadness become depression, fear become an anxiety disorder, and intrusive thoughts become OCD?

If we don't attempt to distinguish normal abnormality from abnormal abnormality, normal anxiety or sadness may be taken too seriously or real abnormality may be taken too lightly. Both of these possibilities are potentially harmful. But there is a way to remove much of this confusion, provide some clarity about "tipping points," and therefore be more helpful to people. Let's take sadness as an example and look at four criteria we can use to distinguish between normal and abnormal sadness.

Measure the Degree of the Sadness

Many of us feel sad from time to time, sometimes for no obvious reason. That's just part of life. But sadness does not automatically equal the mental illness of depression. The main questions to ask here are:

How deep is it? How intense is the sadness? Does it come and go quickly, or does it linger for days, even weeks? Does it cause a person to break down in tears or even feel despairing?

How different is it? Have there been times in the past like this? In what ways is this occurrence similar or different? Did the person previously get better on his own within ten to fourteen days?

How constant is it? Is it erratic, or does it come and go at predictable times of the day, the month, or the year? Are there certain triggers, or is it constant?

These questions will help us measure the degree of sadness and whether it is so abnormal that further action is required.

Measure the degree of sadness
to measure the danger of the sadness.

But what about when there really *are* sad things in our life? Does that not have to be taken into account? Yes, the circumstances of our lives are important to weigh as well.

Consider the Circumstances of the Sadness

In everyday life, we can all expect that there will be days when we experience sadness due to truly sad circumstances and situations. We therefore want to ask the following questions:

Has there been a painful loss? Have we lost a job or a loved one? Have we (or someone close to us) lost our health? Have we lost a friend, or hopes for the future?

Has there been a painful disappointment? Have we been let down by someone? Have we failed or been failed by someone? Have our dreams for our marriage or our children turned to ashes?

Has there been a painful event? This may be something that's affected you directly, or it may be a painful event in a family member or even nationally (school shooting, terrorism, etc.) or internationally (wars, famine, etc.).

If we answered no to these questions, then our sadness is more likely to be serious depression, as there was no obvious reason for it.

If we answered yes to any of these questions, it's more likely that we are experiencing normal sadness. Such everyday losses, disappointments, and suffering start a grieving process, which passes through various stages before we regain a sense of balance or stability in our everyday functioning. While painful, letting this process run its course is helpful in the long run, and we don't want to cut it short unnecessarily. Our response should be to rely on God's grace and help in our time of need, and he will restore our joy in his good time.

If we cut short all sadness
we cut short spiritual growth.

So if everyone faces great loss, disappointment, and suffering in life, and most of them get sad and then recover, at what point does the sadness become abnormal? That's where consideration of the length of time the sadness has lasted becomes significant.

Calculate the Duration of the Sadness

If there has been a loss or a disappointment, we will want to look at the timescale involved. Helpful questions include:

How long has the sadness lasted? When did the loss or painful event occur? The loss of a beloved wife or husband or child will obviously produce longer-term sadness than the loss of a distant cousin. But even if it is an extremely painful loss, the person usually returns to "normal" within three to six months.

How long does the person feel "down"? In all bereavements there will be times when even the most buoyant of spirits will sink for a time, even six months or more after the event. The important question is, how long does the person stay down? A few hours? Days? Weeks at a time?

How recurrent is it? How often do these depressions come around? Every day? Every week? Is there an increasing time gap between them, or is there less of a space than before?

---

*Time sad times and you'll know
when it's treatment time.*

"But aren't there lots of people who have lifelong troubles and they just keep going? Their lives are tough, but they aren't disabled by it? It's about more than the length of time, isn't it?"

That brings us to perhaps the most important criteria when determining if sadness has become a mental illness: what is the impact of the sadness on the person's functioning?

Assess the Impact of the Sadness

What is normal functioning? That's such a difficult question because what's normal for one person may not be normal for another. That's why the preferred term is "stable functioning" rather than "normal functioning." Stable functioning refers to a steady balance or predictability in the everyday functioning of the individual. In other words, there is a consistency in how the person relates to her world, experiences, situations, thoughts, and feelings.

For most of us, there is small variation in our mood or functioning from one day to the next. These fluctuations may be affected by the amount of sleep or exercise we get on any given day, the amount of stress we experience in our home, job, or family relationships, and so on. However, the variations are generally minor and may last only a few days before returning to a stable balance.

Where there is mental illness, a person may have low energy levels, and limited motivation to get out of bed, eat, wash, or interact socially or even connect with their own family. This is not transient but is long-term, chronic, and paralyzing. Stable functioning is impossible.

The most important questions to help us distinguish sadness from depression in such a situation are:

Has it impaired functioning? Is it undermining a person's work, family responsibilities, ability to plan and organize life, etc.?

Has it decreased motivation? Is the will weakened so much that the person can't get excited about anything? Is there a lack of interest in work, hobbies, people, that previously energized him?

Has it diminished energy levels? They sleep and nap a lot, yet no matter how much they rest, they are always tired. Even if there's motivation, there's no ability to follow through. Are they slow in speech, decision-making, actions?

When sadness affects your work,
it's time to work on your sadness.

We hope these four categories of questions will help you discern the difference between normal sadness and abnormal sadness (depression). Follow this model for devising similar questions to distinguish between normal worry and abnormal anxiety.

SUMMARY

Problem: Confusing normal sadness, anxiety, etc., with abnormal sadness, etc., is common and harmful.

Insights: We can distinguish between normal and abnormal sadness, anxiety, etc., by (1) measuring the degree, (2) considering the circumstances, (3) calculating the duration, and (4) assessing the impact.

Action: Distinguish between normal and abnormal sadness and anxiety to measure the seriousness of the problem and get the right help at the right time.

- Use the checklist of three questions presented above to make your own assessment of a loved one.

- Ask someone else in the family for their viewpoint.
- Share the questions with the sufferer to help her discern whether she is depressed or simply sad.
- Ask a doctor or a mental health professional for an assessment.

Tom's Story about Sally

Sally had experienced many life stresses and losses but until now had been able to bounce back after a few days. She had patiently endured her sad life circumstances without falling into deep and lengthy depression.

For the past couple of months, however, she had experienced extreme sadness and fatigue that impacted her ability to experience any joy and to carry on normal life activities. She had to drag herself out of bed in the morning, often feeling more tired than when she had gone to bed the night before. She struggled to concentrate and to be productive throughout her day. She avoided meeting up with friends or even answering the phone, emails, and text messages. This was much too much sadness, and there seemed to be no relief in sight. A psychologist helped her to see that this was no ordinary case of the blues, but rather a clinical depression that required professional help.

5

How Does Mental Illness
Affect the Sufferer?

BECAUSE MOST SYMPTOMS of mental illness are internal and invisible, it can be difficult for others to understand what it's like. Some might even doubt whether mental illness is real, or may perhaps view it simply as the result of sinful choices.

If we could scan or test for mental illness, it would be much easier to understand and explain. Although some scans and tests for some mental illness are becoming available, this technology is still in the early stages of development and is costly. What can we do in the meantime? We can get an internal "scan" of a sufferer's pain by listening for common threads in sufferers' stories and by considering some of the latest medical research. If we do, we will come to realize the following common symptoms of mental illness.

Mental Illness Imbalances Feelings

Especially with affective disorders (those that affect the feelings), sufferers experience intensely painful emotions such as overwhelming sadness, fear, anger, despair, and feelings of worthlessness. As we noted before, although we all experience these feelings from time to time, this is different in length, intensity, and duration. These feelings are so extreme that they imbalance, impair, and even paralyze a person's life.

---

*Extreme feelings
are excruciating feelings.*

These awful feelings are often irrational, meaning they have no logical explanation. That's why people often say to sufferers, "I know you feel bad, and I feel sorry for you, but can't you just think more rationally, and you'll not feel so bad?" Part of the problem with that argument is that sufferers often have impaired reasoning too.

Mental Illness Distorts Thoughts

Although the thoughts are especially affected by cognitive disorders (e.g., schizophrenia), those with primarily affective disorders will almost always find their thoughts messed up too. Their thoughts will tend to be largely negative, often obsessive, usually exaggerated, and sometimes hopeless. They will go round and round the same thing in their mind, usually something sad or painful or fearful, which magnifies it until it squeezes out all other thoughts. This often tends to be an automatic process, meaning it's not something they choose to think about.

Some of the most common thought distortions are:

- *False extremes.* This is a tendency to evaluate personal qualities in extreme, black-and-white categories; shades of gray do not exist. This is sometimes called all-or-nothing thinking. For example, you make one mistake at work and conclude that you are a total disaster.
- *False generalization.* This happens when, after experiencing one unpleasant event, we conclude that the same thing will happen to us again and again. If a young man's feelings for a young woman are rebuffed, he concludes that this will always happen to him and that he will never marry any woman.
- *False filter.* We tend to pick out the negative in every situation and think about it alone, to the exclusion of everything else. We filter out anything positive and decide everything is negative. We get 90 percent on an exam, but all we can think about is the 10 percent we got wrong.
- *False transformation.* Neutral or positive experiences are transformed into negative ones. The depressed person doesn't ignore positive experiences; rather, she disqualifies them or turns them into their opposite. If someone compliments her, she concludes that the person is just being hypocritical or that he or she is trying to get something from her.[1]

People with mental illness may also be affected by intrusive thoughts, obsessive thoughts, distraction, indecision, and so forth. And remember, unlike external causes of pain like a hot stove that can burn us, we cannot retreat from mental pain. It's inside our body or brain. With a tortured mind, there's nowhere to run or retreat to. Thoughts follow us and are with us wherever we go.

---

1 For more on these cognitive distortions see David D. Burns, *Feeling Good: The New Mood Therapy* (New York: HarperCollins, 2012), 54.

We can run from a murderer
but not from our minds.

Those of us on the outside might think, "Well, if it imbalances feelings and distorts thoughts, how come my loved one is so tired and is always going to the doctor?" That's because damaged thoughts and feelings also end up damaging our bodies.

Mental Illness Damages Bodies

God made us in such a way that our thoughts and feelings are tied up with our bodies. Our bodies are affected by our thoughts and feelings and vice versa. We see that in Psalm 32, and 51, and in Proverbs 14:30 and 23:7. It's not a coincidence that illness often follows bereavements, or that diseases like arthritis and even cancer can follow times of prolonged stress. Similarly, when we have the flu or even just a bad cold, our feelings also get down and our thoughts become foggy.

We therefore shouldn't be surprised that, when our thoughts and feelings are so disordered, it hurts the body too. Physical illness such as back pain, digestive problems, exhaustion, headaches, palpitations, insomnia, and others, are commonly found together with mental illness.

Some of the latest medical research has found that depression not only results in more brain tissue loss than Alzheimer's, but also causes significant degeneration of other bodily systems, leading to problems such as coronary disease, diabetes, stroke, and osteoporosis. Patients with untreated depressive illness lose approximately seven years of life. Increased cortisol, a growth hormone secreted in times of stress or fear, affects every cell in the body.[2]

One of the reasons why so many physical symptoms accompany mental illness is that sufferers often experience sleep deprivation. They can't get to sleep, or they wake up early, or wake up repeatedly, or just have a poor quality of sleep. Modern science has proven that sleep deprivation to that degree is extremely bad for both physical and mental health.

Invisible mental illness
causes visible physical illness.

We hope you're beginning to understand how serious mental illness is, and how it affects the sufferer. Maybe it also explains why the person is not as sociable or engaged as before, because, obviously, with all this going on, relationships are impaired.

Mental Illness Impairs Relationships

When people have mental illness, we can expect them to withdraw and become isolated. They don't want to be around people, even people they love and who love them. They don't feel that they have anything to contribute to society and don't believe anyone can help them. Socializing exhausts them and may even scare them. Their church attendance drops, and Christian fellowship is avoided. They stop good activities like sports and

---

2   See the following article, which summarizes and links to recent scientific research: David Murray, "Can Depression Be Cured? Recent Research," October 16, 2016, https://head hearthand.org/blog/2016/10/14/can-depression-be-cured-latest-research/.

hobbies and start actions that only make them feel worse (e.g., binge-watching TV, surfing the Internet, overspending, drinking alcohol, etc.).

Although friendships can be a great source of help to them, they can't summon up the energy that friendship requires. They may even imagine everyone hates them and can feel misunderstood or even persecuted—so much so that they think their families would be better off without them. Obviously, such an illness also affects their relationship with God, but that's such a large and important subject, we will devote the whole of the next chapter to it.

When people can't relate to what's inside,
they can't relate to people outside.

SUMMARY

Problem: As most symptoms of mental illness are internal and invisible, many people doubt the reality of mental illness or view it primarily as sin.

Insights: From listening to stories and scientific research, we learn that mental illness (1) imbalances feelings, (2) distorts thoughts, (3) damages bodies, and (4) impairs relationships.

Action: See inside a sufferer to grasp the reality and torture of mental illness.

- Read books or blog posts about the pain of mental illness.
- Listen to your loved one's story. Ask about how the mental illness has affected each of the four areas listed above.
- Take time to imagine what it would be like to live with this pain inside.

Many Stories

Here's a sample of stories from #thisiswhatdepressionfeelslike on Twitter:

- Too numb. Wish I could hurt. Wish I could feel. Next day: Too much pain. Wish I were numb. @bachbunny

- It's raining, all the time. But you still have to do things, and it's sunny for everyone else. @RobertVore

- The alarm clock immediately fills me with dread. I battle the desire to call in sick or cancel plans. @therealjonpress

- Showering, getting dressed, then sitting on the bed. For 8 hours. Repeat. @whatthezem

- Too tired to stay awake, too tired to go to sleep. @selenawand2

- Imagine a black hole physically placed in your chest which constantly sucks life energy out of you and prevents energy from reaching your body, while an inner voice constantly tells you that you won't manage. @andreasgerden

- Your brain is the video game and someone else controls it. @angelopanuncio

And here's my own:

- One big minus in my heart stretching into every area of life. @davidpmurray

6

How Does Mental Illness
Affect Spiritual Life?

HOW DOES MENTAL ILLNESS affect a person's spiritual life? There are two mistakes we can make when thinking about this question. First, when mental illness is a sickness, it is a mistake to condemn such suffering as sin. Such misclassification turns a sufferer into a sinner, heaps false guilt on the person, and multiplies her suffering.[1] Second, and just as damaging, is when mental illness is even partly caused by personal sin but is blamed on sickness alone. In this case, false comfort may be offered, turning a sinner into a sufferer, and depriving the person of the healing power of repentance and faith in Christ.

As serious confusion and consequences accompany both of these mistakes, it's imperative that we try to get this right. So how does mental illness affect our spiritual lives? We'll begin by noting how different facets of our humanity impact each other.[2]

---

1 "Labeling a mental illness as only a 'spiritual issue' is not helpful, and it can be detrimental" (Lifeway Research, *Study of Acute Mental Illness and Christian Faith*, 5, https://research.lifeway.com/wp-content/uploads/2014/09/Acute-Mental-Illness-and-Christian-Faith-Research-Report-1.pdf).

2 Mental health experts interviewed by Lifeway emphasized that, while they spoke in generalities in these interviews, "when they are in a room with a patient, it becomes very specific to that person" (*Acute Mental Illness and Christian Faith*, 3).

Spiritual Life Is Impacted by Thoughts, Feelings, Body, and Relationships

The example of sleep deprivation and its impact on our thoughts, feelings, bodies, relationships, and souls, can help us understand the impact of mental illness on our spiritual health. Having said that, although sleep deprivation has some bad consequences, the consequences of mental illness are far worse.

Thoughts Impact Spiritual Health

If you've been sleep deprived for a few days, you know how fuzzy and slow your thinking can become. Simple problems become like algebra. Eventually, hallucinations can occur, where we see things that are not really there. Such a mental slowdown or confusion will obviously impact our spiritual life.

Similarly, mental illness reduces our capacity to think and perceive accurately. Clear and rational thought is difficult. The ability to distinguish between truth and error is severely hindered. Our imaginations and perceptions play tricks on us, and we can become delusional. As God usually works through the mind and uses our perception, reasoning, and mental processing, if these abilities are impaired, then so too will be our relationship with God.[3]

Feelings Impact Spiritual Health

Just as sleep deprivation affects our thoughts, it can also destabilize our mood directly and indirectly. Our disordered thoughts produce disordered feelings. Some get angry, others get weepy. All of us become unpredictable as mood regulation is challenging.

---

3 "Twenty percent of individuals with acute mental illness agree their mental illness made/makes it difficult to understand salvation" (*Acute Mental Illness and Christian Faith*, 6).

When we are exhausted, it becomes impossible to lift ourselves emotionally, to motivate ourselves, and to love our closest friends and family. Negative feelings such as fear and discouragement are multiplied. We cannot separate our spiritual life from such influences.

Mental illness does the same kind of thing to our feelings. We can feel very little, or our feelings are all over the place. We lose motivation and enthusiasm for life and for people. Anxiety and depression overwhelm us. We can be up one moment and down the next. A disordered mood is always going to disorder our souls. When we feel down in general, we are going to feel down spiritually. When we are despairing of life, it's inevitable that we will despair of our spiritual state. Anxiety and depression disturb our inner peace—interfering with our prayers, our Bible reading, and our perceptions of God.

The Body Impacts Spiritual Health

Research into sleep deprivation has discovered that it impacts not only our brains and our nervous system but also our major organs and our immune system. It even impacts us at a cellular level, with more than seven hundred genes being changed by a week of sleep deprivation.[4] God made us in such a way that our bodies affect our souls. Think of how having a common cold limits spiritual liveliness. Our souls are not disconnected from our bodies. We are not disembodied spirits.

As we saw in chapter 5, recent research on mental illness has found that it also causes serious damage to our bodies, upsetting our body chemistry and changing the shape and functionality

---

4   David Murray, *Reset: Living a Grace-Paced Life in a Burnout Culture* (Wheaton, IL: Crossway, 2017), chapter 3.

of our brains.[5] This physical damage will usually also impair our spiritual lives.

Relationships Impact Spiritual Health

For most people, especially men, sleep deprivation vastly increases the likelihood of conflict. We get grumpy, impatient, and bad-tempered. We withdraw from social situations and have no time even for close friends. We just want to be left alone. If we don't want to be with people or talk to them, it is unlikely we will want to be with God or speak with him.

Mental illness tends to have a similar effect. When our thoughts, moods, and physical health are disordered, it is almost impossible for that not to injure our relationships. As our most important relationship is with God, we can expect that mental illness is going to undermine that relationship in a similar way.[6]

Causes and Consequences

Do you see how mental illness has rational, emotional, physical, and relational consequences, and therefore great spiritual consequences as well? When mental illness is a sickness, most spiritual symptoms are the *effects* of mental illness, not the *cause* of it.[7] Understanding this will help us avoid turning sufferers into sinners, moving us from condemning to comforting.[8]

---

5   Again, see the following article, which summarizes and links to recent scientific research: David Murray, "Can Depression Be Cured? Recent Research," October 16, 2016, https:// headhearthand.org/blog/2016/10/14/can-depression-be-cured-latest-research/.

6   "Unhealthy faith expressions can actually be a symptom of mental illness. Look for behaviors outside the norm of the group" (Lifeway Research, *Acute Mental Illness and Christian Faith*, 5).

7   Mental health experts remind us that "Strong faith does not make a mental illness go away" (*Acute Mental Illness and Christian Faith*, 5).

8   "Depression was mentioned the most often as being directly impacted by situations, personal care, friendships, and spiritual life" (*Acute Mental Illness and Christian Faith*, 3).

> *There would be no depression*
> *if there were no sin,*
> *but not all depression is*
> *caused by personal sin.*

Does it go the other way too? Yes, it does. Our spiritual life affects our thoughts, feelings, bodies, and relationships and, if unhealthy, it can be the cause of mental illness.

Spiritual Life Impacts Thoughts, Feelings, Body, Relationships

Thankfully, not every sin results in mental illness. If it did, we would all be mentally ill all the time. The kind of sin that God may chastise with mental illness is usually serious and stubborn sin that remains unrepented of. In our counseling experience, we have noticed that the kinds of sins that cause depression are gross sins, defiant sins against light, addictive sins such as pornography or alcoholism, and sins of long-term bitterness or anger.

A biblical example of sin-caused depression is King David's experience after he committed adultery with Bathsheba and murdered Uriah (2 Sam. 11–12). Psalms 32 and 51 reveal the inside story of these sins. While outwardly David continued to rule and perhaps managed to put on a good face, inwardly he was in a terrible state. His thoughts were dark and depressing. His feelings were negative, anxious, and obsessive. His body was affected with pain and exhaustion. He lost his appetite and ability to sleep. He could not face God, and sensed that God had withdrawn his favor from him. This is a "perfect" example of depression and anxiety resulting from sin and reverberating into every part of one's being.

In David's case, it is important that we do not turn him from a sinner into a sufferer. Rather, we must trace the cause of his mental and emotional disorder to his sin. That's why the prophet Nathan brought a message of conviction and condemnation, not one of comfort and sympathy. It was only when David repented, following Nathan's confrontation with him, that a measure of joy, peace, and health returned.

If we rule out the cause of sin,
we rule out the cure of repentance.

The relationship between mental illness and spiritual life is complex and demands prayerful and careful thought. Having said all that, though, it's encouraging that "88 percent of family members in a household of someone with acute mental illness agree their mentally ill family member is fully able to make a decision to follow Christ and grow in that faith."[9]

SUMMARY

Problem: Many mistake the relationship between mental illness and a person's spiritual life, leading to inappropriate condemnation of sufferers, or inappropriate comfort of sinners.

9 *Acute Mental Illness and Christian Faith*, 6.

Insights: Spiritual life is impacted by our thoughts, feelings, body, relationships, and vice versa.

Action: Distinguish between disorders that result from sickness and those that result from sin in order to offer appropriate comfort or conviction.

- Think through how your last physical illness influenced your spiritual life.
- Consider how serious sin shapes your thoughts, feelings, relationships, etc.
- When trying to decide if a mental illness is the result of sin, ask yourself these questions:
  - Is there serious sin in the person's life?
  - Is the sin defiant, stubborn, and persistent?
  - Is it unrepented of?
  - Are steps being taken to prevent repetition of the sin?

David's Story

If I've learned anything through helping people with depression and anxiety, and through suffering it myself, it's how complex human nature is. Previously, like many Christians, I had mistakenly adopted a dualistic view of human nature. To put it simply, dualism says that the body is here, and the soul is there, and never the two shall meet. You can do what you like with your body, and it won't affect the soul, and vice versa. When I eventually realized that the body and soul were inseparably intertwined and interconnected, it helped me to better discern when mental illness was the result of sin or a sickness, and when it was a bit of both. Although we might prefer the simplicity of dualism, the complexity of human nature is not only true but is the key to helpful counsel and direction.

7

How Does Mental Illness Affect Those around the Sufferer?

MENTAL ILLNESS AFFECTS not just the sufferer but also those around him, most of whom are not prepared for it. In the absence of a diagnosis, this begins with confusion about what's happening to the sufferer and usually mutates into anger about his irrational and harmful words or actions. When a diagnosis is made, people will often despair of any recovery or perhaps have false hopes of a very speedy recovery, neither of which helps anyone.

Is there any way we can prepare for this, or prepare others for it? Is there a way for people around the sufferer to handle the onset of mental illness better? Yes and yes. Here are three insights to prepare us for this and to help us handle it better.

There Are Four Main Groups Affected

Let's think about the effects on families, friends, the workplace, and church.

The Family Is Affected

This, of course, is usually the first place where the cracks become evident in a person's mental health. It's also the place where she has the most impact, due to her proximity to others and the amount of time she is at home. The family bears the brunt of a sufferer's withdrawal, sadness, anger, or confusion, and also feels the pain of this more keenly because of the changes in someone they love so much. Lifeway found that "parents of children with mental illness deal with a substantial amount of denial and grief."[1]

Friends Are Affected

If you're a friend, you will wonder if you've offended the sufferer. He withdraws from you. Phone calls are not returned. He becomes unpredictable and erratic. He's not much fun to be around anymore. Perhaps he is hypercritical, moody, aggressive, or self-focused.

The Workplace Is Affected

Many people can still hold down a job while suffering from mental illness, but their performance is often impaired. They may take more days off work than before and be late to work or meetings. They might be in conflict with a number of colleagues or clients. They tend to bring a dark mood into work with them, and people may feel a bit scared around them.

The Church Is Affected

Just as at work, the church attendance and involvement of people experiencing mental illness may be inconsistent and unpredictable.

---

1   Lifeway Research, *Study of Acute Mental Illness and Christian Faith*, 4, https://research.life way.com/wp-content/uploads/2014/09/Acute-Mental-Illness-and-Christian-Faith-Research -Report-1.pdf.

They may be disturbed during services or leave the service abruptly. Usually there is little desire to pursue fellowship, and excuses are made to avoid people.

We cannot see mental illness,
but we can feel its many impacts.

That's quite a "ripple-effect," isn't it? It's more like a "tsunami-effect." There's hardly any area of life untouched when mental illness erupts. So, when might we expect these changes to start appearing? Immediately and all at once, or slowly and in installments?

There Are Three Main Stages in the Effects

We want to look at what usually happens before diagnosis, at diagnosis, and after diagnosis.

Before Diagnosis

This is a time marked by confusion, anguish, and misunderstanding. The sufferer is not herself, there's clearly something wrong, but no one knows what it is. Whether it's a slow or a sudden onset, the end result is the same: bewilderment, frustration, embarrassment, and disorientation for everyone concerned. What is going on? Why is she acting so odd? Why is she drinking?

At Diagnosis

When a person is finally diagnosed with a mental illness, there can be some relief and clarity. At last we understand what's going on. However, that's often short-lived as everyone realizes what is involved. There may be trials of different medications, expensive weekly counseling, perhaps even inpatient hospitalization. Time off work may be required, and perhaps constant supervision at home. Some family and friends still won't accept or understand it, due to ignorance or prejudice. Some might withdraw because of fear or embarrassment. Some can despair, thinking that the person will never be "normal" again.

After Diagnosis

After the initial days of treatments and interventions, there are a lot of adjustments required as various steps are often needed to care for the person and adapt to the new "normal." As there are rarely any quick fixes, it soon sinks in that this is going to be a longer period of suffering than might have been expected. Sometimes sufferers may struggle with compliance, which can often create frustration for those around them. This can be a heartbreaking time.

In the long-term, many sufferers return to normal health, especially if they comply with medical advice and counseling. However, some relationships can take a while to heal due to some of the pains and wounds that may have been inflicted during the illness. Lengthy periods of peace, which gave hope that normality was returning, may be dashed by sudden and unexpected flare-ups. Life is then lived in the shadow of the possibility of another episode.

Others do not return to normal. The mental illness can turn out to be a lifelong struggle to one degree or another. This obviously has lifelong implications for families, friendships, employment, and church life.

---

*Mental illness is often slow to develop
and even slower to cure.*

So what are the main effects on those around the sufferer?

There Are Three Main Effects to Manage

The most common effects of mental illness on family and friends are confusion, denial, and anger.

Confusion

It's bewildering to see a person we knew and loved acting so un-usually, so out of character. We see changes that alarm us, and we worry about what is going on. We may speculate and arrive at the worst conclusions.

Denial

When we begin to consider the possibility that a person has mental illness, or even after getting a professional diagnosis, we may fight against accepting it. We find it hard to believe what we are seeing or hearing. This might be the last person you thought would suffer in this way. "It must be something else." Sometimes this denial might take the form of getting numerous tests to try and find another cause. We don't want to face up to the possibility, and consequences of, accepting this diagnosis. Denial can take the form of false hope. "It's not that bad," or, "It can be quickly fixed." Denial is often the result of embarrassment, or the fear of the person or your family being stigmatized.

Anger

Although most illnesses produce a lot of sympathy, mental illness can also cause a lot of anger. We may be angry with the person. That may be righteous anger if he has brought the illness on himself through drug use, overwork, sin, etc. But it can often be unrighteous anger, blaming the person for the illness in a way that you wouldn't blame him for any other illness. Or you can be angry with God for doing this or letting this happen. You can be angry with yourself for not seeing it sooner, or maybe you even blame yourself. It can be a time of great despair and can even result in our *also* falling into depression and anxiety.

---

*Wrong responses to mental illness
can cause more mental illness.*

Confusion, denial, and anger are common stages in grieving a bereavement. However, unlike with the death of a loved one, with mental illness there is no finality. So how can we respond in a better way?

There Are Three Main Ways to Respond Better

If we want to respond better, we need to think about three areas: education, submission, and service.

Education[2]

Reading this book and educating yourself about mental illness should help to mitigate common responses that do much harm. You will be able to recognize the symptoms and take appropriate steps such as getting a professional evaluation. You will not panic. You will realize how common this is and how many things can be done to mitigate or heal mental illness.

2 See the comments in our first footnote in chapter 1, above.

Submission

Accepting God's will in the matter is an important part of a healthy response. We stop fighting and denying. We bow down and say, "Not my will, but your will be done." We also need to submit to the person's limitations and adjust accordingly. This is the only way to silence torturous questions like, "Why me?" or "Why them?"

Service

This is what God has called us to. Mental illness may be a long-term problem and therefore it's best if we frame it as one of the primary areas in which we serve God, rather than as an inconvenience that may hinder our service to God. It is an opportunity to glorify him as a family member, as a friend, as a pastor, as an employer, as a colleague, and so on.

Good responses to mental illness
produce good results from mental illness.

SUMMARY

Problem: People are not prepared for the way mental illness affects others around the sufferer.

Insights: The four main groups affected by someone's mental illness are impacted in multiple ways and go through several stages in their initial response, but, with the Lord's help, they can learn how to respond in a spiritually beneficial way.

Action: Understand and prepare for the common effects of mental illness upon others so that you can process it better and turn it for spiritual profit.

- Consider ways that you and others have responded badly to mental illness among family, friends, at work, or in church.
- Write down some reasons why you or others have reacted in this way.
- Confess this to people you have hurt or stigmatized in the past and seek their forgiveness.
- Think about what a submissive spirit would look like and pray for that.
- View serving the mentally ill as part of your Christian service.

Tom's Story about Scott

When Scott's parents (see chapter 3) arrived to pick up their son from the college residence hall, they were angry. How could their son become so irresponsible as to not turn in assignments and refuse to attend his classes? How did his dorm room become such a disheveled and disorganized mess? How come he sat in silence as they peppered him with questions during the two-hour car ride home? They wondered if he had become involved with a negative crowd. Had he started taking drugs?

In the following weeks, their anger gave way to confusion and perplexity as nothing they tried seemed to break through

Scott's apparent guardedness and defensiveness. He was still isolating in his room and apparently sleeping most hours of the day and night. It never occurred to them that their son might be dealing with a mental illness rather than a phase of life or an attitude problem. While his parents focused only on the symptoms (or manifestations of the illness) rather than attempting to discern what these symptoms meant, their frustrations turned to anger, in effect multiplying their own sorrow and distress. When they began to consider what was motivating these symptoms, they were able to seek and receive help for both Scott and themselves in their journey through mental illness.

8

How Do People React to
Having Mental Illness?

A PERSON WITH MENTAL ILLNESS will often resort to defenses that stop her from getting the help she needs. Such defenses are not based on reality, prolong and deepen the suffering, and delay necessary treatments and interventions.

It is important to recognize and understand these defenses so that we can move sufferers toward a healthier response that will make them open to treatment. Let's begin by briefly considering the speed of onset, because that's often a significant factor in the way a person responds.

The Reaction Is Influenced by the Speed of Onset

For most people, the symptoms of mental illness appear slowly and gradually, over months, and maybe even years. Changes in mood and actions are often so subtle and imperceptible that there's no real awareness of what's happening in their thoughts, feelings, and actions. They (and we) may write it off as, "I'm having some tough days," or, "Perhaps this will pass, so I should not pay too much attention to it," or, "I shouldn't make such a big deal out of something that hopefully is nothing," or, "I'm just not feeling like my old self."

On the rare occasion that the onset is sudden, it's more obvious and often results in alarm, panic, and fear, in both the person and those around him. But in these cases too, the reaction can be something like, "It's just a blip," or, "I'll be back to normal tomorrow."

Sudden mental illness produces sudden responses,
slow mental illness produces slow responses.

What's the most common reaction to expect from someone with symptoms of mental illness?

The Reaction Is Usually Defensive

Whether the onset is slow or sudden, the person will often try to find ways to explain away the problem. These rationalizations are called defense mechanisms because they erect mental barriers to accepting the reality of the situation.

In general, defense mechanisms are the way that most of us will attempt to defend ourselves when confronted with something that feels emotionally or psychologically threatening. In the physical realm, it is relatively easy to predict and identify the instant physical reactions to physical threats. These reactions are generally referred to collectively as the fight, flight, or freeze reaction. We may stay frozen in place (freeze), try to run away (flight), or confront the threat (fight).

Emotional reactions to emotional threats are more difficult to detect, discern, or explain. It is important to attempt this, though, because, while these emotional defense mechanisms may seem to provide a sense of safety and emotional insulation from the threats, they do so in a very temporary and limited manner. If left to continue long term (more than a few hours or days), they can ultimately harm a person and prevent him from seeking the proper treatments and counseling that are necessary to allow the healing to begin.

Some of the most common defense mechanisms are listed below. But remember, sometimes a person may be using a number of them, even in one conversation.

Denial

This happens when a person does not want to admit there could be a problem, often because she doesn't want to concede what she may perceive as weakness. Internally, the person may tell herself, "This is not and cannot be happening." In conversation, she denies that anything is wrong or that there have been any changes going on in how she thinks, feels, or interacts with others.

Minimizing

Minimizing the severity of a problem is also very common. A person is aware that there is a problem but does not want to admit the full extent of the problem and therefore downplays it. He doesn't want the problem to exist, he doesn't want to seem overly concerned, and he doesn't want others to be overly concerned. A typical minimizing response is, "This is no big deal."

Avoidance

An avoider will tell herself, "This is too big to handle!" There is a realization that there is a problem but uncertainty as to what she should do or what should happen next. Most of us will try to avoid what we don't know how to deal with. Whether it's a relational problem or a challenging home repair project, we procrastinate and make excuses. However, not only does the problem not go away, but it usually grows in magnitude . . . as does our anxiety about handling the project.

Suppression

A person recognizes that there is a problem but makes a conscious decision to suppress or push down the feelings that he is having. A typical response is, "I don't want to talk about it." Usually, the suppressor is closer to being able to deal with a problem than the avoider, but, overwhelmed by the amount of conflicting thoughts and feelings, he attempts to squash the feelings and thoughts. He is hoping that, by suppression, the issue can be dealt with "some other time."

Isolation

When a person has some realization that her thinking and moods are no longer under her own control, the urge to "go into hiding" becomes strong. She doesn't want others to get close enough to realize that something is wrong. She gradually begins to drop out of regular activities and interactions with others. She may not realize she is doing this or why, excusing it as, "Just not feeling up to it today," without realizing that her world is becoming smaller and smaller. In extreme cases, the person may refuse to leave her house or even her bed.

Rationalization

Here, a person tries to come up with alternative explanations, or justifications are made for his disturbing symptoms, feelings, and irrational thoughts. Sometimes this is also known as excuse-making or blaming. For example, a depression may be blamed on "others pressuring me," or, "You would not be doing so well if you had to go through what I'm dealing with." Sometimes excuses can be deflected back toward the person raising concerns: "What about you? You think you're doing better than I am?" Sometimes the justifications are quite illogical and therefore easy to see through; other times, they can be subtler and even put the other person that is lovingly raising concerns on the defensive.

Sometimes there is the assumption that something is wrong medically; this is more helpful, as it usually drives people to seek care and proper diagnosis. However, even in this circumstance, many will not automatically suspect mental illness is the culprit causing distress.

---

*Defending ourselves
damages ourselves.*

So, if these are wrong and damaging reactions, what is the right reaction to the onset of mental illness, and how do we move a person toward the right response?

The Reaction That Honors God Is Acceptance

Acceptance rather than defense is what we want to get to. Acceptance involves prioritizing truth and evidence above our wishes and emotions. Acceptance is embracing reality for what it is rather than what we want it to be. Acceptance opens a person up to receiving the help and assistance of others that will lead to proper treatment and the stabilizing of what can be a debilitating illness.

So, what does this look like in practice? It usually involves asking the sufferer for permission to start a conversation about where he is at and what you are seeing. That can take the form of asking questions or talking about what you've observed. Maybe you can note how the person is, compared to how he used to be. Perhaps you can talk through possible explanations and rule some out. Ultimately the aim is to move the conversation to a more objective and external evaluation by a doctor or counselor, so that personal feelings and relationships don't cloud the issue.

It's very important that loved ones broach this subject, raise this possibility, and ask these questions in a gentle, caring, and kind manner, rather than in a panicky, emotional, threatening, or condemning manner. Perhaps you could begin with the illustration of what we would do if we saw numerous bruises on someone's skin. That is, we would ask questions, we might get medical tests if there was no obvious explanation, and so on. Then we can move into what we are sensing in a person's mood and mind.

It's best not to say, "You're depressed," or, "I think you're mentally ill." Rather, it's best to start a conversation by highlighting a couple of things that concern you. It may take a while for a person to come to full acceptance, but even just sowing the seed-thought can, over time, remove defenses and promote honesty.

And, of course, if a loved one comes to you with her own questions and concerns about herself, then do not dismiss those concerns. Take them seriously, and deal with the worries in a truthful and careful way. The way you react will determine whether the person continues to talk or just bottles it up.

Remember, pain is God's usual way of alerting us that there is a problem that deserves attention and care. This is true of physical pain and also of emotional pain. To ignore or to minimize pain gives the illness a free pass to continue and become worse, delaying treatment and increasing recovery time.

Accepting mental illness
accelerates mental health.

SUMMARY

Problem: When symptoms of mental illness arise, the sufferer often resorts to defenses that delay the necessary treatments and interventions.

Insights: The reaction is influenced by speed of onset, the reaction is usually defensive, and the reaction that honors God is acceptance.

Action: Identify common defense reactions and work toward acceptance to speed up help.

- Pray that God would give honesty, truthfulness, transparency, and courage to all concerned.
- Ask God for wisdom and gentleness in raising concerns with a loved one or hearing *his* concerns.

- Take your time and space the conversation out over some weeks if the person is resorting to defenses.
- Prepare the ground by sharing articles or talking about mental illness in general.
- Be ready to offer reassurances in order to prevent or overcome defenses. For example:
  - Mental illness doesn't mean you're a bad Christian or that you lack faith.
  - This does not mean you're crazy or that you'll lose your job.
  - This is common in a fallen world, and therefore you're not weird.
  - I don't think less of you, in fact I admire your courage, and will support you at every step.
- Identify common defenses and discuss them as they arise.
- Get an objective outside assessment.

David's Story

Delay, deny, defend. That basically sums up my own reaction to my depression. Looking back, I now see that I have had low-grade depression for most of my adult life but had gotten so used to it that it just felt normal. However, the multiplication of major life stressors during a short space of time in my early fifties multiplied and deepened my depressive tendencies.

Even I could tell that I was in trouble, but when my wife, Shona, asked me from time to time, "Are you okay, David?,"

I continued to delay, deny, and defend. Eventually Shona pointed out that I was bringing her and my family down too, and pleaded with me to see a doctor. By that point, I knew in my heart that something was wrong, but I was still stunned that, after a detailed assessment, my doctor diagnosed me with severe depression and moderate-to-severe anxiety. It was a good shock, though, because I couldn't argue with these objective facts, and it opened my mind to taking it seriously and doing something about it. I went from delay, deny, defend, to assessment, acceptance, and action.

9

What Are Some Common Hurdles to Recovery?

WHEN MENTAL ILLNESS IS RECOGNIZED and the problem admitted, there are still a number of hurdles on the way to successful treatment. These hurdles come at the beginning, in the follow-through, and in the long-term. At any point of these stages, successful treatment can stumble and fall, preventing or slowing down recovery, and even setting a person further back than they already are.

The First Hurdle Is Getting Early Treatment

When any illness is ignored and left to itself, it has free rein to grow and to silently do its devastating work. Some cancers are not recognized until they are at an advanced stage. The symptoms came on so gradually that they were not noticed. As the symptoms began to increase, they were mostly ignored or minimized and no calls were made for medical attention. It wasn't until the cancer had done significant damage or had completely taken over the person's body that medical attention was sought.

Refusing to ignore changes in a person's health is key in early detection and treatment of mental health symptoms. Making the decision to speak up and to seek help, particularly with mental health concerns, takes courage. Breaking the code of silence and secrecy in order to reach out for assistance is perhaps the biggest step that can be taken in the treatment of a mental health disorder. The size and seriousness of this hurdle is seen in the statistic that only about a third of people with an anxiety disorder seek treatment, although, when left untreated, anxiety often leads to depression as well.

Some delay treatment due to shame or fear of talking about their struggles with a stranger. Some worry that their struggles will not be kept confidential. Others may be afraid of being "locked up." For men, the hurdle is usually higher due to imbalanced cultural norms of masculinity and a reluctance to form relationships for emotional and mental support.

The longer the denial,
the longer the distress.
The sooner the treatment,
the shorter the torture.

Once a person is able to recognize their condition and admit their need, they're over the first hurdle. What's the second hurdle?

The Second Hurdle Is Consistency of Follow-Through

Some who suffer with mental illness are tempted to drop out of treatment prematurely, especially when they do not feel better immediately. The first set of medications may not work, or there may be unpleasant side-effects. The person may not be able to find a Christian counselor, or may not hit it off with the counselor assigned to her. Perhaps the counselor probes some sensitive areas that the person does not want to talk about. Others drop out when there is some relief of the symptoms (some pain relief) but before stabilization has taken place.

As in any other illness, discontinuing care before the person is medically cleared usually limits or harms recovery. Take, for example, the antibiotics that our doctor gave us for that sinus infection. The instructions were to take the pills for ten days; however, by day five, we started to feel better and decided we no longer needed the prescribed treatment. By the third day off the medication, the symptoms were returning with a vengeance. Many of us have been there and done that, and it didn't work out very well. It's the same for a person with a mental illness.

Follow-through is particularly challenging for mental illness because effective healing often takes a long time, and it's hard to persevere with slow-acting meds and long-term counseling. When counseling is involved, insurance may run out after a certain number of visits. New habits of exercise, sleep, or eating often slip, and old patterns return.

When treatment is working
keep working on the treatment.

But even when a person is enabled to get over the first hurdle of getting early treatment, and the second hurdle of follow-through, there's a third hurdle that appears on the track.

The Third Hurdle Is Long-Term Maintenance

The final hurdle is follow-through with long-term maintenance strategies. Once a person is feeling better, the temptation is to hope the illness will never return. Statistics do not support this theory; rather, in the case of depression, for people who have been diagnosed with major depressive episodes, the likelihood that they will have a recurrence is about 10 percent. Some place the statistics even higher. For example, Dr. William Marchand, a clinical associate professor of psychiatry at the University of Utah School of Medicine, said that the risk of recurrence—relapse after full remission—for a person who's had one episode of depression is 50 percent. For a person with two episodes, the risk is about 70 percent. For someone with three episodes or more, the risk rises to around 90 percent. Marchand, therefore, advocates designing and implementing a prevention plan, which not only can prevent recurrence but can shorten and reduce the intensity of any times that the depression does return. Some suggestions to consider are outlined below in the action section.

The key to success in all of this is acceptance, which Dr. Lauren Mizock defines as "actively recognizing and managing the symptoms of a mental health problem."[1] It is admitting and coming to peace with the fact that long-term management of the illness is needed to maintain a stable life.

If maintenance is our mission,
we'll lengthen remission.

---

[1] Lauren Mizock, "Five Tools That Help Women Accept a Mental Health Problem," *Psychology Today*, July 17, 2017, https://www.psychologytoday.com/us/blog/cultural-competence/201707/five-tools-help-women-accept-mental-health-problem.

SUMMARY

Problem: Even when mental illness is admitted, there are still three hurdles to recovery in the short, medium, and long-term.

Insights: (1) The first hurdle to recovery is getting early treatment; (2) the second hurdle is follow-through; (3) the third hurdle is long-term maintenance.

Action: Recognize the hurdles to recovery and take steps to overcome them with short-, medium-, and long-term strategies. Work with the sufferer and professionals to develop a prevention plan. Consider areas such as:

- Medication organization and accountability.
- Reduced but regular counseling (once a month, or once a quarter).
- Keep a journal that measures moods (happy/sad; anxious/peaceful) and mind-sets (negative/positive; confused/clear).
- Record sleep, eating, and exercise.
- Be sensitive to changes.
- Be aware of vulnerabilities.
- Take extra precautions during stressful times.

Tom's Story

"I am too busy to deal with this right now. I mean, I have all these deadlines and responsibilities, and people are relying on me right now." That was my response when my wife, Ruthanne, raised concerns about my deteriorating mood. She challenged me: "How can you help others when you can't even take time to help yourself?" And she was right. During a time of "harsh providences," as I referred to them, I was falling behind in my work at home, at church, and in my job (as a counselor!). I knew very well that everyone is susceptible to depression but did not consider that now the helper needed help. Recognition of "this is my experience" was my biggest hurdle; reaching out to others for assistance was the second biggest hurdle.

10

What Causes Mental Illness?

WHAT CAUSES MENTAL ILLNESS? That's one of the most important questions we can ask when considering this problem. However,
as the multiple wrong answers prove, there is widespread ignorance
and confusion about the causes of mental illness. This only magnifies and deepens the problem because it results in wrong diagnosis,
wrong treatment, and wrong blaming.

How can we learn to think correctly about the causes of mental
illness, so that we diagnose it correctly, treat it properly, and stop
blaming people for something when it is not their fault? We can
do so by looking at the three main causes of mental illness: what
we are (we have wrong biology), what we do (we have wrong lives),
and what others do to us (others wrong us).

We Have Wrong Biology

Mental illness can be caused by what we are physically. Our biology
can play an important role in the problem.

God Created Everything Good

When God made us, he made us good. We were perfect in every
way. Nothing was wrong with us in any way. We were physically,

emotionally, mentally, spiritually, and relationally perfect (Gen. 1–2). If Adam and Eve had not sinned, we would never have known what depression, anxiety, bipolar disorder, or schizophrenia were.

Sin Has Broken Everything

But our first parents did sin, and we now know these disorders all too well. How did that happen? God warned Adam and Eve that if they disobeyed him, they would die. That did not mean they would instantly drop dead, but that death would enter their systems and they would begin to weaken and wither in every way. That's exactly what happened when they sinned (Gen. 3:6–19).

God also cursed the earth on account of their sin, meaning that it began producing thorns and thistles, causing humanity sweat, toil, and tears. But that outward curse and brokenness was replicated in Adam and Eve themselves. It was a mirror of what had happened to them.

Sin Has Broken Our Genes

When death entered humanity, it altered our perfect genes and made us susceptible to damaging changes, diseases, and so on. Our genetic makeup mutated in various ways, being passed down to us by parents whose own genes were similarly deformed. Our bodies also became vulnerable to various diseases and hostile external forces. Every bodily system is damaged when we are born and is vulnerable to further damage as we grow. Our brains are broken, and so is every system that interacts with them. As our brain is the most complicated organ in the body, we shouldn't be surprised that mental illness can affect us. For example, there is research showing that schizophrenia is possibly connected with autoimmune disorders.[1] Also, research-

---

1 "Interesting New Research in Schizophrenia," http://www.goodmoodbadmood.com/blog/new-interesting-research-in-schizophrenia; and "Could Psychosis Be an Autoimmune

ers have found common genetic factors in five mental disorders.[2] Interestingly, even the seventeenth-century Puritans distinguished between depression which had physical causes and those which had spiritual causes.[3]

Having said this, it's also important to remember that, although our genetics are influential, they are not determinative. Just as when someone has cancer, not everyone in their family will contract it, so it is with mental illness. That said, awareness of our genetic vulnerabilities is important.

What we are
connects with what we feel.

Does that mean that we are just victims, that this is something that just happens to us, that we have no responsibility? No, we can actually bring mental illness upon ourselves.

We Have Wrong Lives

Although we should normally not consider this cause first, we must acknowledge that our sinful attitudes, desires, and actions can cause or at least contribute to mental illness.

Disease?" *BBC*, February 26, 2018, https://www.bbc.co.uk/ideas/videos/could-psychosis-be -an-autoimmune-disease/p05zdl33?playlist=rethinking-mental-health.

2 "Common Genetic Factors Found in 5 Mental Disorders," *National Institutes of Health*, March 18, 2013, https://www.nih.gov/news-events/nih-research-matters/common-genetic -factors-found-5-mental-disorders; and "Do You Inherit Your Parents' Mental Illness?" *BBC*, May 10, 2016, https://www.bbc.com/news/magazine-36228055.

3 David Murray, "The Puritans and Mental Illness," *HeadHeartHand.org*, http://headheart hand.org/blog/2013/05/08/the-puritans-and-mental-illness/.

The most common spiritual causes of mental illness are addictions, immorality, greed, overwork, bitterness, anger, hatred, pornography, idolatry, and sinful thought patterns. We'll come back to thought patterns shortly, but let's think a little about why these other sins can cause mental illness.

First, there can be a physical element to this. For example, substance abuse is going to damage our bodies and especially our brains. So is overwork, due to the wear and tear on our bodies and brains. Anger, hatred, and bitterness also cause our stress response system to operate at excessive levels, raising inflammation in our bodies and altering our chemistry as well as damaging other bodily systems. There's considerable evidence of what damage excessive digital technology is doing to our brains and our nervous systems. Overeating, undereating, and eating badly can also contribute.[4]

Second, there's a spiritual element to all these sins, and other sins that do not have a physical element (e.g., sinful thought patterns) can also damage our mental health. The shame and guilt that accompanies these sins troubles our conscience, makes us fearful and sad, and drives us away from God. God also can distance himself from us as a chastisement for our sins.

Third, we can adopt sinful thought patterns, false thinking that can result in depression and other mental illnesses. As we'll see below, these can also be the result of things people do to us, and not only the patterns that we choose and develop ourselves.

So, yes, we can blame Adam for some of our troubles, but we have to blame ourselves at times as well. This is why it is so important to get objective outside assessment of our mental health. With-

4   "Can What You Eat Affect Your Mental Health?" *Washington Post*, https://www.washington post.com/national/health-science/can-what-you-eat-affect-your-mental-health-new-research -links-diet-and-the-mind/2014/03/24/c6b40876-abc0-11e3-af5f-4c56b834c4bf_story.html.

out such outside help, we may not be able to judge our situation correctly. Or, we may be so hardened by sin that we refuse to take any blame. There's also the possibility that we may be so mentally ill that we blame ourselves for things that others are responsible for.

When we do bad,
we can expect to feel bad.

So, what might others be responsible for when it comes to mental illness?

Wrong Is Done to Us

I'm sure we all know somebody who had a brain injury caused by a car accident that resulted in their personality being changed temporarily or even permanently. Brain scans can show the part of the brain that is damaged.[5]

Research now reveals that we don't need to be in a car accident to suffer brain damage. Physical and sexual abuse, especially at a young age, can also change the size, composition, and connectivity of the brain, resulting in changes not only in our thoughts but in our feelings as well. While some of this can actually be reversed with professional interventions, it can rarely be completely cured, leaving some with mental and emotional vulnerabilities. Just as we wouldn't blame someone for not running when they have a broken leg, we must not blame people who have had their brains broken by the sin of others.

5   Andrew Fountain, "The Brain Revolution," November 20, 2017, http://nlife.ca/brain.

It isn't just physical and sexual abuse that damages us; so does verbal abuse. It not only can change our brains physically, it can also change the way we think and our sense of identity. For example, if someone has had hypercritical perfectionist parents who have told them they will never be good enough, it's not surprising if that becomes their default thinking pattern. If someone has been bullied and mocked for years, they're going to think they're worthless. If someone has grown up being told of all the terrible, dark, and dangerous things in the world and being exposed to violence in reality or in movies, it will be no surprise if they are anxious and fearful.

Again, with skillful counseling, due to the plasticity of the brain, some of these harmful thought patterns can be changed. The brain can be rewired. But we must not blame such people in the same way that we might challenge others who by their own choices have become mentally ill.

When we suffer from bad people,
we may suffer with bad feelings.

SUMMARY

Problem: Without knowing the causes of mental illness, we may take the wrong actions.

Insights: Mental illness may be caused by (1) original sin, (2) our sin, or (3) others' sins.

Action: Identify the causes of mental illness in order to take appropriate action.

- Take some time to consider the role each of these three categories of causes have played in a sufferer's life.
- If it's a mix of factors, try to gauge the proportion each has played.
- What's the right reaction to each of the three causes?
- Even if you don't suffer from mental illness, consider how each of these areas have affected your life.

David's Story

I'm still trying to fully understand all the factors that contributed to my own depression. Scottish genes, weather, and culture were the low starting point. Abuse excavated a deeper hole. Deeply sinful teen years followed by deep conviction of sin plunged me even deeper. Even when I embraced the gospel, my church culture was negative, legalistic, and joyless. Overwork and performancitis sunk me gradually and imperceptibly lower over many years. Painful injustice at work, followed by a summer of sleeplessness due to prolapsed discs in my neck, virtually turned off the lights of my soul. To top it all off, I thought I had killed my frail eighty-four-year-old father in a driveway accident. Although it turned out to be "just" a broken leg, it left me with PTSD and months of flashbacks. Put that together with a negative and self-critical default mind-set, and you have a perfect setting for severe depression and anxiety.

.

11

Can a Christian Have Mental Illness?

SOME CHRISTIANS BELIEVE that Christians cannot have mental illness. If a professing Christian is depressed, anxious, or bipolar, they think it's because they are not a real Christian, or that there is some terrible sin they haven't repented of, or that they need to repent of the depression or whatever the problem is. Nearly half (48 percent) of evangelicals believe that serious mental illness can be overcome with prayer and Bible study alone.[1]

The result of this condemnation of mental illness as sin is that many Christians do not admit they have a mental illness, they don't talk about it, and they don't reach out for help. If they do reach out, they will often turn to the secular world instead of the church, because they sense they will get more understanding, sympathy, and help there. However, secular approaches can sometimes lead to further spiritual difficulties and complications.

---

1   "Mental Health: Half of Evangelicals Believe Prayer Can Heal Mental Illness," Lifeway Research, September 17, 2013, https://research.lifeway.com/2013/09/17/mental-health -half-of-evangelicals-believe-prayer-can-heal-mental-illness/.

If we want to overcome these challenges, we need to understand three reasons why Christians can suffer with mental illness.

Christians Can Have Mental Illness Simply because They Are Human

Christians have broken bodies. A Christian's body is just as fallen and weak as any other person's body. That means they can have heart attacks, diabetes, Alzheimer's, and, yes, mental illness. Their brains can break, their chemistry and electricity can malfunction, their hormones can be imbalanced, and so on.

Christians live in a broken world. Christians are not shielded from the effects of living in a fallen world. We have accidents, we are abused, we are wronged, we are lied about. People hurt us, some intentionally, some unintentionally. We see and hear sad and painful events and stories that traumatize us. We lose loved ones. Our families break up. Trauma has been shown to change the shape, size, and functionality of the brain and other bodily systems that are related to how we think and feel.

Christians get stressed. We are designed to function for short amounts of time under high stress and then to return to calm and more relaxed functioning. But when our bodies and minds are under stress for long periods of time, our God-given stress-response system (our "fight or flight response system," as noted earlier) can malfunction. When we are confronted by some sort of threat (real or perceived, physical or emotional), a small structure in the back of our brains (the amygdala) takes over in order to respond to and survive the perceived threat. This works really well when we are confronted by an external threat (e.g., a dangerous animal). Our bodies respond, as they were designed, to eliminate or to withdraw from the threat. We either fight our way to safety or run away from the threat. Once we have gotten to safety, the amygdala's survival function is no longer required and relaxes; now the front part of the brain (rational and calm thinking) can again take over; the body and the brain can relax.

However, when a person feels under constant threat, when there is no relief from the threat, stress, or pressure, the amygdala remains activated. It takes over the pleasure centers of the body and brain (limbic system), producing excessive and continuous amounts of the stress chemicals adrenaline and cortisol. Eventually, these chemicals attack the internal organs and overall health of the person. While these chemicals are fine in short and small doses, when sustained for a long time they can become extremely dangerous to our physical and mental health.[2] Stress can also trigger an underlying vulnerability to mental illness that may not have been activated in calmer circumstances.

*As long as Christians remain
part of humanity,
they will suffer like the rest of humanity.*

We hope you are beginning to see that Christians are just as human as everyone else and therefore suffer and get stressed like everyone else. But you might wonder, does mental illness ever come to believers as a result of personal sin?

---

2   Anjali Chandra, "Fight or Flight: When Stress Becomes Our Own Worst Enemy," *Harvard Science Review* 20, no. 1 (December 3, 2015), https://issuu.com/harvardsciencereview/docs /hsrfall15invadersanddefenders. https://harvardsciencereview.org/2015/12/03/fight-or-flight -when-stress-becomes-our-own-worst-enemy/.

**Christians Can Have Mental Illness
because They Are Sinners**

In the previous chapter, we noted how personal sin can cause depression through physical and spiritual damage. But there are two additional reasons why Christians in particular may experience mental illness.

First, there's the divine chastisement that's reserved for God's children, as King David found out when he committed adultery and murder! Psalms 32 and 51 reveal the depression and anxiety that David felt while living in unconfessed sin. Of course, as noted in chapter 5, if God chastised us with mental illness every time we sinned, we'd all be depressed all the time! Thankfully, in his mercy, he does not do that. However, if our sin is especially serious or we are stubbornly unrepentant in it, God may afflict our minds and emotions to get our attention and make us seek his mercy and grace. God's discipline, then, is to teach us how bad sin is and to draw us back to himself. So, though painful at the time, it is ultimately for our good.

Second, the absence of Christian virtues and graces can also damage our moods and our minds. For example, if we are not praying, if we are not reading our Bibles, if we are not consciously growing in God-centered faith, love, hope, patience, trust, and worship, these deficits may eventually cause mental, emotional, and spiritual damage. Worry and anxiety will take the place of trust and confidence; independence and self-control will replace dependence and God's control; working for acceptance with God will take the place of trusting Christ for acceptance with God; and a secular identity will replace a Christian identity. All these replacements carry emotional and mental costs which, over time, can result in mental illness.

> *As long as Christians continue to sin,*
> *Christians will continue to suffer.*

"But surely," one might say, "Christians have less mental illness than non-Christians?"

Sometimes, it's just the opposite.

Christians Can Have Mental Illness because They Are Christians

While Christians have more resources to combat mental illness than non-Christians, they can also have more vulnerability to it than non-Christians. We can see that in three ways.

Christians are especially targets of the devil. While the devil targets all people, he especially hates God's people (Gen. 3:15). He hates them because they used to be his, and he wants to get them back. He wants to destroy their happiness in Christ. He therefore attacks them with greater ferocity and will do all in his power to damage them. Battling against such spiritual warfare is hot and stressful. It takes a toll on us in many ways, including on our thoughts, emotions, and even our bodies. The devil tempts us and tests us in ways that he doesn't tempt and test non-Christians.

Christians are especially conscious of their sin. One of the effects of the Holy Spirit in our lives is to show us our sinfulness. We see the evil in our own hearts more than ever before. That can be scary and depressing, especially if we don't bring the gospel to bear upon these dark and discouraging experiences. We also get cast down at our weakness in the face of temptation and because of the little progress we're making in the Christian life.

Christians are especially affected by all the sin and suffering in the world. When we are brought to Christ by his grace, and as we become more like Christ, we are tenderized in our hearts and made more sensitive to evil in the world. We see people's sins in a new light, especially the sins of loved ones, and we grieve over the disorder that sin causes. We see tragedies, wars, terrorism with increased agony because of the suffering inflicted, and especially because people are being swept into eternity without the gospel.

Do you see how being a Christian can make mental illness more likely? However, as we said earlier, we also have more resources, as we shall be discovering later in the book.

---

*Christianity can be a crown of thorns
more than a bed of roses.*

SUMMARY

Problem: The denial that Christians can have mental illness leads to condemnation, isolation, and seeking secular help.

Insights: Christians can have mental illness (1) simply because they are human, (2) because they are sinners, or (3) because they are Christians.

Action: Admit that Christians can have mental illness, that sometimes it's not their own fault, and understand how some factors outside their control make it more likely.

- Think about times when illness has impacted your thoughts and emotions.
- Next time you're stressed, notice how it affects you mentally and emotionally.
- Instead of jumping to the conclusion that mental illness is always caused by sin needing repentance, start with the assumption that it's simply suffering that needs sympathy and support.
- List the kinds of questions you would ask someone to discern what proportion of their mental illness is the result of sin they should repent of.

David's Story

The first paragraph of this chapter describes me. At seminary I was taught that Christians should not have mental illness, and if they do it's because they need to repent of sin. I confess that I was among the 48 percent of evangelicals who believe that serious mental illness can be overcome with prayer and Bible study alone. Even though my first two pastorates were in the Scottish Highlands, where rates of depression are among the highest in Europe, I still had no understanding or sympathy for Christians who suffered in this way.

It was only when it came not just close to home, but into my home, that I was forced to abandon my false assumptions and deal with reality. My godly, cheerful, extrovert, Type-A wife plunged into a long depression that began during her fourth pregnancy. It took many conversations and a lot of reading to abandon my simplistic and dualistic view of mental illness and understand it more holistically and accurately. Over some months, I was forced to acknowledge my dangerous ignorance and embrace the fact that Christians get depressed too. It was the beginning of new usefulness in my ministry as people detected greater understanding and compassion and began to seek my help and counsel.

12

What Role Do Pastors Have in Helping the Mentally Ill?

A PASTOR FACES two main challenges when it comes to caring for Christians with mental illness: he may be the first person to be contacted with a mental health problem,[1] or he may be the last person people contact![2]

When he's contacted first, the pastor is sometimes expected to have all the answers and provide all the care and counsel. However, there are limits to a pastor's availability and expertise. On the other hand, when he's contacted last, he is then excluded from an important role in guiding, counseling, caring, and helping.

1   Fifty-nine percent of pastors have counseled one or more people who were eventually diagnosed with an acute mental illness (Lifeway Research, *Study of Acute Mental Illness and Christian Faith*, 5, https://research.lifeway.com/wp content/uploads/2014/09/Acute-Mental -Illness-and-Christian-Faith-Research-Report-1.pdf).

2   Lifeway found that "(1) people with mental illness often turn to the church first for help; (2) church has an opportunity to be a place of healing; (3) pastors' reactions to people struggling with mental illness are varied; (4) pastors need to understand their own limitations; (5) walking with the mentally ill can benefit the congregation, not just the individual; (6) pastors are most likely to change their view on mental illness once they are personally impacted by it" (*Acute Mental Illness and Christian Faith*, 4).

So how do we get this right, so that pastors don't end up doing either too much or too little? Let's see what role pastors have in caring for the mentally ill.

Pastors Teach the Congregation

As one of the pastor's roles is to teach the word of God, he can help those with mental illness in two ways when doing this.

General teaching about doctrine and life. The first way a pastor cares for his flock is by feeding them the word of God. A steady diet of gospel-saturated food will help to prevent mental illness and also play a role in curing it. The faithful preaching and teaching of God's word over the long-term will nourish and strengthen the flock and therefore increase their overall health, including their mental health. If a Christian does suffer with a mental illness, it becomes even more important that they continue to receive good spiritual food as part of a package of care.

Specific teaching on mental illness. In addition to general teaching and preaching of the Bible, the pastor should from time to time also speak about mental illness in particular.[3] Topical addresses based on the word of God, or applications of texts in a preaching series, or seminars on mental illness are all invaluable in raising awareness, reducing stigma, and building a culture of care. Although 65 percent of family and friends and 59 percent of sufferers want their church to talk openly about mental illness so that it is not so taboo, 66 percent of pastors admit that they have spoken about it in sermons or in large group messages only once a year. Forty-nine percent of pastors rarely or never speak to their church about mental illness.[4]

---

3 "Sixty-six percent of pastors have read several books on counseling people with acute mental illness" (*Acute Mental Illness and Christian Faith*, 16).

4 *Acute Mental Illness and Christian Faith*, 8.

Understandably, some pastors feel ill-equipped to do so, but they can bring in trained people to speak, or perhaps recommend resources.[5]

Personal testimony about mental illness. One of the most powerful therapeutics is for pastors to talk about their own struggles with mental illness. Nearly one in four pastors admit that they have personally struggled with mental illness.[6] Most pastors who have admitted this, and have encouraged transparency in their congregations, have become much more useful to others with mental illness.

Sensitive preaching opens the way
to sensitive pastoring.

Is pastoral care all done in the pulpit or at the lectern? No, it's also done in the closet.

Pastors Pray for the Congregation

A pastor is to give himself to the ministry of the word and to prayer (Acts 6:4). This second pastoral role can be fulfilled both publicly and privately when it comes to mental illness.

Pastors pray for prevention of mental illness. Just as we pray for God to protect us and our flock from cancer and strokes, so we should pray that he would protect our minds from mental illness.

---

5 Lifeway's research highlighted that "people with mental illness or their families deal with a large amount of shame and social stigma," and therefore "honest conversations that bring clarity to the topic are needed," and these "conversations about mental illness need to change in frequency and tone" (*Acute Mental Illness and Christian Faith*, 4).

6 Sarah Zylstra, "1 in 4 Pastors Have Mental Illness," *Christianity Today*, September 22, 2014, https://www.christianitytoday.com/news/2014/september/1-in-4-pastors-have-mental-illness-lifeway-focus-on-family.html.

Pastors pray for those with mental illness. It's a strange fact that, despite so many people in our congregations suffering with depression and anxiety, and despite mental illness being the main cause of disability, we hardly ever pray about it in public. However, it is incredibly encouraging for sufferers to hear pastors and elders praying for those with depression and anxiety just as normally as they do for others getting surgery or getting old.

Pray for the caregivers—professional and personal. Caring for the mentally ill can be exhausting and frustrating. We therefore want to pray for all who are involved in this: trained professionals in the medical field, and also those who care on a personal and familial level. Pray for their patience, perseverance, encouragement, and relief.

> *Prayer for the mentally ill*
> *is power for the mentally ill.*

So, pulpit and closet. Is that it? Does the pastor ever actually meet with individuals suffering in this way?

Pastors Shepherd and Counsel Individuals

A pastor can shepherd individuals with mental illness in three ways.

The pastor will shepherd before the onset of mental illness. The pastor is not just reactive but proactive. He doesn't just shepherd the sheep when they get into trouble. He shepherds them before trouble comes. He therefore keeps his eyes open for warning signs of things like depression or anxiety in his flock. If he knows of a family history of mental illness, he can help those with such vulnerabilities to preempt mental illness, and even prepare for it, as much as possible. He guides people to take preventative steps and models that himself.

The pastor will shepherd by counseling those with mental illness. According to Lifeway, one in four pastors are reluctant to get involved in cases of acute mental illness because of the challenges involved.[7] However, we want to encourage pastors to get involved, within certain limits. When a Christian comes to their pastor with mental illness, the pastor will want to give general spiritual counsel and advice to begin with. He will also want to ensure that the person goes for a medical check-up. While the limits of time usually mean that the pastor cannot be the main counselor for the person, he should assure him that he will stay with him throughout and will get him all the help that he is able to provide through other resources.

The pastor will shepherd by praying with the person. Even if the pastor is not the main counselor, he will often be his main prayer partner. Regardless of how serious the problem is, the person needs prayer and will need it going forward. Sometimes, praying with a person is the very best thing we can do for him.

---

*A pastor must give spiritual counsel
and arrange for supplementary counsel.*

If a pastor doesn't do everything, who does the rest?

[7] Lifeway Research, *Acute Mental Illness and Christian Faith*, 5. However, that's a minority view, as 74 percent of pastors strongly disagree that they are reluctant to get involved with those with acute mental illness because previous experiences strained their time and resources.

Pastors Are Part of a Team of Pastors

Thus far, we have used the word "pastor" in the traditional sense of the man called to preach the word in the congregation, who is usually paid as a full-time employee. However, one of the biggest steps we can take to improve care for the mentally ill in our congregations is to leave the traditional definition of "pastor" behind, and instead adopt a biblical definition of the term. When we turn to the Bible, we find that the church is to be shepherded by a team of elders, who are also called pastors and overseers. Yes, one of these elders or pastors is usually called to preach full-time, but all the pastors/elders are called to teach, govern, and shepherd the flock. Adopting this biblical definition means that the pastoring and counseling are shared between all the elders/pastors, it engages all the pastors/elders' gifts, and, though most elders are not full-time pastors, they are more permanent pastors than most full-time pastors (thus providing more long-term continuity of care). So, below, when we're using the word "pastors" we're using it in the biblical sense of a team of elders. What, then, should such pastors do?[8]

Pastors spend time with the mentally ill. We suggest these permanent pastors be given the main responsibility to care for the mentally ill (no more than one per pastor/elder) and that this pastor be asked to spend an hour every week or two with the sufferer. This regularity and accumulation of time and experience is critical for assessing the spiritual state and health of the sufferer. They will see those suffering at their best and at their worst.

Pastors recognize their limitations. Pastors generally have had very little training in how to counsel the mentally ill. This is especially the case if it's clinical depression, an anxiety disorder, or one of

---

8 Pastors should involve mature Christian women when counseling a female member.

the rarer disorders such as schizophrenia.[9] What should pastors do in these circumstances? It is vital that pastors recognize both how much and how little they can do. This will vary from pastor to pastor. While all pastors should be encouraged to educate themselves and get training in this area, the level of time and expertise required will often limit their usefulness, and they should recognize that.[10] This is not to be an excuse to opt out of all care and counsel, but to do as much as possible within one's limitations and capacities.

Pastors involve other Christians. Ideally, pastors should be trained in specific areas of counseling (e.g., depression, anxiety, conflict, etc.) or work toward equipping other members in these areas. This will prevent the pastor who usually does the majority of the preaching from being overwhelmed with counseling needs. It also gives consistency of care, as the main preaching pastor will probably be called elsewhere eventually, and therefore is generally not the ideal person in the congregation to provide long-term care.

Pastors get help from other experts. Sometimes, mental illness can require help from outside the church in addition to (not instead of) the care of those within the church. In Lifeway's survey, it was found that 68 percent of pastors say their church provides care for the mentally ill or their families by maintaining lists of experts to refer people to. However only a quarter of families are aware that their pastor has such a list of resources.[11] Over time, pastors should be reaching out into their local community of caregivers and

---

9 Fifty percent of pastors indicate they don't personally know anyone who has been diagnosed with schizophrenia (*Acute Mental Illness and Christian Faith*, 14).

10 Most do. "The majority of pastors indicate they could be more equipped to identify when to refer people to medical professionals" (*Acute Mental Illness and Christian Faith*, 17).

11 *Serving Those with Mental Illness* (Colorado Springs: Focus on the Family, 2014), 15, https://media.focusonthefamily.com/pastoral/pdf/PAS_eBook_Series_Mental_Health _INTERACTIVE.pdf.

professionals to identify reliable and skillful people whom they can involve in caring for the mentally ill. Ideally these counselors and professionals will be Christian, but that is not always necessary if the counselor is willing to work cooperatively with the pastor and within clear parameters. Regardless of whether it's a purely medical issue or not, the pastors will want to be involved especially with spiritual aspects of the care.

> *A pastoral team*
> *prevents pastoral burnout.*

SUMMARY

Problem: The pastor may be either the first person or the last person to be contacted with a mental health problem. If he's the first person, he may be overwhelmed with the number and complexity of cases. If he's the last person, he may have little if any voice in the person's life.

Insights: Pastors (1) preach and teach the congregation about mental illness; (2) pray for those with mental illness; (3) shepherd and counsel individuals about the spiritual elements of mental illness; (4) are part of a team of pastors.

Action: Pastors should encourage and accept an important but defined role in raising awareness of mental illness and in teaching, caring for, and arranging counseling for the mentally ill.

- If you're a pastor, start praying for those with mental illness and mentioning it in prayer.
- If you've suffered with mental illness yourself, consider referring to it or talking about it in a sermon.
- Encourage others in the congregation, especially elders and mature Christian women, to be trained in counseling those with mental illness.
- Build a network of trusted medical professionals and counselors in your area.
- If you're a church member, encourage your pastor to speak about mental illness.
- Provide your pastors with good books on the subject.

David's Story

I'm often invited to speak in churches and at conferences about the Christian approach to mental illness. Often, a few weeks after such events, I get emails or calls from pastors telling me that they've had more counseling opportunities in a few weeks than in all the previous years of their ministries. They are usually asking me how to get further training, and also how to train their elders and others to share the load.

Opportunities also arise when a pastor discloses his own struggles with mental illness. One of my pastor friends never mentioned depression and anxiety in his prayers or preaching. Then he fell into a deep depression which meant he was off work for a few months. When he returned, he didn't try to hide what he'd been through, but from time to time spoke about his experience and how much he had learned from it. The result? Again, many people came out from the shadows and disclosed their own struggles to him, opening up multiple opportunities for gospel ministry and care. He soon realized that he needed to share the load, and over a number of years arranged basic training about mental illness for his fellow-elders and others in the congregation.

13

What Role Does the Church Community Have?

CHRISTIANS OFTEN THINK that mental illness is something only for experts, and certainly not something with which the church in general, nor they in particular, can help. This is a mistake that can lead to a number of damaging consequences. First, it can mean that Christians are not trained to deal with mental illness either in themselves or in others. Second, people are afraid of mental illness, and hesitate to help. Third, Christians make mistakes in their attempts to help people with mental illness, adding to their suffering.[1]

While none of us are ever going to be experts in this field, we want to show you what the church family can still do to serve people with mental illness.

---

1   "The response of people in church to individuals' mental illness caused 18 percent to break ties with a church and 5 percent to fail to find a church to attend" (Lifeway Research, *Study of Acute Mental Illness and Christian Faith*, 7, https://research.lifeway.com/wp-content/up loads/2014/09/Acute-Mental-Illness-and-Christian-Faith-Research-Report-1.pdf). Seventeen percent of family members in a household of someone with acute mental illness say their family member's mental illness impacted which church their family chose to attend (*Acute Mental Illness and Christian Faith*, 7).

The Church Family Unites with Each Other

Just as the church family gathers around and supports families who have serious illness or have suffered bereavement, so the church family should gather around to support the mentally ill. Like other trials and afflictions, mental illness in a family member should bring the family together in loving and practical concern.[2]

Therefore, instead of running from those with mental illness or avoiding them, let's run after them and accept them.[3] Seventy percent of people with acute mental illness would prefer to have a relationship with people in a local church through individuals who get to know them as a friend.[4] If you're scared or reluctant, ask God to give you a heart and a mind for the mentally ill. Find out who they are in the congregation. Notice who rushes away quickly or stands on their own on the periphery. Bring them in and include them in conversations and activities. It takes a lot of intentionality and effort to befriend the mentally ill.

One skill we need to develop is the ability to listen. Don't run in with solutions, but ask questions such as, "How are you feeling?" "What are you thinking?" "How has your week been?" Listen carefully and attentively; sufferers have usually developed sensitive antenna for those who ask but then don't listen.

2 "Before sharing their illness with others, it is important for the individual to feel they are in a safe church or group" (*Acute Mental Illness and Christian Faith*, 5).

3 *Serving Those with Mental Illness* (Colorado Springs: Focus on the Family, 2014), 16, https://media.focusonthefamily.com/pastoral/pdf/PAS_eBook_Series_Mental_Health _INTERACTIVE.pdf.

4 "Social support and community in the local church is important for personal spiritual growth" (Lifeway Research, *Acute Mental Illness and Christian Faith*, 5). Fifty-six percent of pastors, 46 percent of family members in a household of someone with acute mental illness, and 39 percent of individuals with acute mental illness strongly agree that local churches have a responsibility to provide resources and support to individuals with mental illness and their families (*Acute Mental Illness and Christian Faith*, 8).

When you decide it's time to speak, do so gently, quietly, and caringly. Try to avoid judgments and criticisms. Focus more on encouragement. Share Bible verses that focus on God's love and salvation. Given how much mental illness isolates people and makes them feel unloved and unwanted, deepening the illness, don't underestimate the power of including them and welcoming them in the church family.[5]

---

*Mental illness cuts off,
but the church family connects.*

So, we've spoken to them. What about speaking to God *for* them?

The Church Family Prays for Each Other

The most important thing we can do for sufferers is to pray for them and pray with them. Pray for them before you meet them, during meetings with them, and after meeting them. It's often hard for depressed and anxious people to pray and, therefore, if you can encourage them to join in your prayers, that's going to be a help for them. Pray slowly, with pauses, and give them opportunity to make your prayers their own, either verbally or silently. Let them know that you've been praying for them and will continue to do so.

---

5 "Fifty-three percent of individuals with acute mental illness say their church has been supportive. . . . Among individuals with acute mental illness who attended church regularly as an adult, 67 percent say their church has been supportive. Seventy-five percent of family members in a household of someone with acute mental illness say their church has been supportive" (*Acute Mental Illness and Christian Faith*, 7).

Pray for and with the family and friends of those with mental illness. If the church neglects the mentally ill, it is perhaps even more guilty of neglecting those who care for them day after day. Those who live with the mentally ill carry a heavy burden of care and can easily get dragged down themselves. So, encourage them by reminding them that you pray for them, and also pray with them for strength and patience. Pray for both sufferers and those who care for them in public prayers (mentioning names only with permission).

Mental illness may stop a person praying
but it starts the church praying.

We've listened to them, we've spoken to them, and we've spoken to God for them. What about *doing*?

The Church Family Cares for Each Other

Be patient. Realize that there is no quick fix. We need to be in this for the long haul. There are going to be ups and downs, disappointments and frustrations. This is a long-term commitment, and therefore a service more suited to long-term members rather than those just passing through or pastors, who are usually temporary and transient.

Be sensitive. We need to be very careful in our language. We try to avoid condemning or criticizing as much as possible. Sometimes we must rebuke or direct, but we try to do so having built a strong foundation of love and support, and in a way that's constructive.

Be an advocate. Let's encourage our churches to care for the mentally ill. They are members of Christ's body, and we are called to bear their burdens (Gal. 6:2). Provide information in leaflets and in book form to raise awareness and acceptance. Perhaps we can set up a support group where they can meet with others who suffer as well as those who have recovered, to share, learn, and encourage one another.[6]

Be a counselor. Each congregation could train a male and a female to do biblical counseling for those with mental illness. Although sufferers will often have their own professional counselors, they can benefit from caring, wise Christians who regularly share the Scriptures personally with them. It's not a substitute for professional counseling but can supplement it. For mild to moderate anxiety and depression, biblical counseling may be all that some people need. This training and equipping takes a while but is a valuable long-term investment for the whole church.

Be an enabler. So far, we've looked at ways we can serve the mentally ill. But one way to serve them is to help them to be servants. We serve them by helping them to serve. Involve them in your ministry or give them simple tasks to do around the church. Given that many feel useless and worthless, helping them to feel useful and valuable again is great medication.

We serve the mentally ill
by helping them to serve.

---

6 Sixty-nine percent of individuals with acute mental illness indicate churches should help families find local resources for support (*Acute Mental Illness and Christian Faith*, 8).

Do you see how much we can do to care for the mentally ill? This is not something that should just be left to the pastor. It's an area in which all the members can be exercising their gifts for the edification of the body.

SUMMARY

Problem: The church often thinks that mental illness is something only for experts. This can lead to church members being untrained, fearful, and sometimes even harmful in dealing with fellow believers who are suffering such illness.

Insights: The church family (1) unites with each other, (2) prays for each other, and (3) cares for each other.

Action: Unite with, pray for, and care for the mentally ill.

- Think about why you may be afraid of or avoid those with mental illness.
- What mistakes have you made in your relationships with people who have mental illness?
- Who is suffering with mental illness in your church family?
- What kind of prayers and Bible verses can help sufferers?
- What caring role can you have in the lives of sufferers?
- What can you do to equip yourself to care for sufferers better?

Tom's Story about Cheryl

Craig and Brad were elders in their local church. For months they had been struggling to understand how to relate and minister to Cheryl. For years Cheryl had been intermittent in her attendance at worship. She would also frequently have anger outbursts and engage in power struggles with other church members. Elder visits seemed to be of little effect in producing positive change. During some of these visits, there were times she would seem contrite and ready to make changes; sadly, these changes were short-lived.

At their wits' end, Craig and Brad reached out to me for assistance. Instead of a highly confrontational approach to their elder work, they were able to approach Cheryl with a firm gentleness and a willingness to "hear her out." Through this, they learned of her diagnosis of a mental illness and were able to enlist the assistance of several sisters in the congregation as special friends to assist Cheryl in better navigating relationships and church life.

14

What Role Do Family and Friends Have?

FAMILY AND FRIENDS are the "boots on the ground" when a loved one has a mental illness. They are vital and necessary parts of the healing team.

However, they can also become part of the problem. Family and friends can feel overwhelmed, frustrated, and burned out. They have been caring for their loved one for so long, they feel as if they have nothing left to give. They then become emotionally distant or cold, and even physically withdraw from the family member. The sufferer inevitably notices this and feels to blame for the emotional strain. As the sufferer is unable to accurately perceive what's happening, he can also begin to withdraw both emotionally and physically, sometimes blaming others for withholding love, affection, and support.

Having said all that, family and friends can also become part of the solution and be more helpful than harmful.

Family and Friends Know the Sufferer Best

They knew the sufferer before. Family and friends have been with, known, and loved the sufferer before he became ill. They have been committed to him throughout his life and will continue to be so. That existing relationship is a massive asset, given how hard it is for the mentally ill to form new relationships, and how suspicious they can be about others trying to help them.

They know the sufferer's soul. This long-term, intimate, personal, and prior knowledge is extremely helpful when it comes to assessing a person's spiritual condition. Those who didn't know the person before he became ill might conclude, based upon his present condition, that he is not a Christian or, at least, that he is a very backslidden Christian. Those who know him best, though, can look back on years of faithfulness, and can also catch glimpses of what they saw before of Christ's work in him.

They love the sufferer most. While other members of the care team can be involved in helping in various ways, there is nothing like feeling loved, and that is something family and friends are especially good at. As a common factor in mental illness is feeling unloved, when the family can make a person know that he is loved, it can be deeply therapeutic.

Lexapro and Prozac can help,
love and patience can heal.

Does that mean we have to do everything? No, the family is only a part, though a big part, of a support team.

Family and Friends Are an Essential Part of the Support Team
Family can do a lot. To start with, try to have a family relationship with the person just as you would with any other member of the

family. One young woman struggling with depression told her father, "I just need you to be my dad. I need you take me out for coffee, to be interested in what is going on in my everyday life, just hang out with me and let me hang out with you." That seems to suggest, "Don't try to fix me," but rather, "Just be my cheerleader, my confidant, my safe place to go when I'm feeling down or insecure and need a listening ear or a shoulder to cry on." If we can do that, we're doing a lot.[1]

The family cannot do everything. Dealing with a short-term or transient illness is completely different from dealing with a chronic illness. The latter takes much more patience, time, and stamina. It may not be always the same, as the illness waxes and wanes. The road to recovery or stabilization is filled with unexpected starts and stops, with unexpected twists and turns. It is a journey that in many cases is long-term, and in some cases, even lifelong. Forming realistic expectations is, therefore, essential in dealing effectively with the illness and in preventing burnout. One of these expectations is that we will need allies in the church family and the health professional community to provide the long-term support needed to sustain us through periods of recovery and relapse.

The family is part of a support team. If sufferers rely only on their immediate family for help and support, they will eventually overwhelm the family with their needs. They will also end up with disappointed expectations. Sufferers need a range and diversity of support. They need friends as well as family. But, just as a chair cannot stand on one

1 Lifeway listed key tools for families: "(1) establish realistic time frames; (2) understand illness isn't going to just 'disappear'; (3) let go of others' expectations; (4) make room in their lives to deal with the illness; (5) establish boundaries that lead to success; (6) understand that it's not about them" (Lifeway Research, *Study of Acute Mental Illness and Christian Faith*, 4, https://research.lifeway.com/wp-content/uploads/2014/09/Acute-Mental-Illness-and -Christian-Faith-Research-Report-1.pdf).

or two legs, neither can a support system for someone with mental illness, especially if it is long-term, as many mental illnesses are. The safest and most supportive chairs have four legs: family, friends, church family, and the health professional community.

---

*The fact that we can't do everything
doesn't mean we can't do anything.*

So how do we get the balance right between offering some support ourselves and relying on a team to provide the rest? The answer is forming realistic expectations.

Family and Friends Need Realistic Expectations

If we want to avoid opt-out or burn-out, creating realistic expectations is vital.

Realistic expectations of themselves. Each member of the family-and-friend circle should try to ascertain to what degree can they contribute to the person's healing. What is reasonable and sustainable? Factors to be taken into account are the severity of the illness on the one hand, and the number, age, temperament, availability, health, and skills of the family and friends on the other hand. A discussion with others who have experience can help with achieving a good balance.

Realistic expectations of others. Talk with other family and friends to try to share the burden and get some kind of plan in place that is going to keep everybody on the same page. Ideally this would be done in a group, with each taking responsibility in certain ways, and with regular reviews for accountability.

Realistic expectations of the sufferer. Ideally, these agreed expectations should also be communicated, explained to, and agreed upon by the sufferer, so that his or her expectations are not raised too high nor are depressingly low.

Great Expectations *is a movie,*
realistic expectations are life.

SUMMARY

Problem: Family and friends can be part of the problem but can also be an important part of the solution.

Insights: Family and friends (1) know the sufferer best, (2) are an essential part of a support team, and (3) need to agree on realistic expectations.

Action: Involve family and friends and guide them in supporting a sufferer.

- If you've been caring for a loved one with mental illness, how would you characterize your relationship with him or her over the years?
- Are you on the burned-out or the opting-out side of the scale? Or are you doing okay?
- How would you assess your loved one's faith over the long term? What's missing that used to be there? What's present that's always been there?

- Which family and friends are part of your support team? Have you agreed on a plan of support?
- What is a reasonable and sustainable contribution you can make? Factors to be taken into account are the severity of the illness, the number, age, temperament, availability, health, and skills of the family and friends.
- Where do you need to adjust your expectations?
- How can you help your loved one adjust his or her expectations?

Tom's Story about Cheryl

"Loneliness" was the word Cheryl used to describe her struggle with mental illness (story continued from chapter 13). "I didn't understand," she explained, "so how could I expect anyone else to get what I was dealing with?" Before Craig and Brad's compassionate engagement, she was ready to give up on church and social involvement.

They were able to assist Cheryl by getting her engaged in a women's Bible study and a care group; this led to personal relationships with other ladies and then with families in the congregation. Being involved with these ladies, she had phone numbers of other supportive people who were available to talk with her during times of more intense struggle. Eventually Cheryl was able to discern some of her gifts and began to volunteer helping with serving coffee and with fellowship dinners before Wednesday night prayer meetings.

Everything changed when she was able to get reconnected to mental health treatment and was able to build trusting relationships with "my handlers," as she described them. These were family and friends committed to being available to be with her and assist her.

15

What Role Do Mental Health Professionals Have?

SOMETIMES, NEITHER FAMILY AND FRIENDS nor the church can manage a sufferer's mental illness on their own. However, when they realize this, and begin to look for help, they often don't know whom or where to turn to. The situation meanwhile can be going from bad to worse. There's also the justifiable fear that getting "worldly help" could do more harm than good. But professional help can be approached and accessed in a way that helps rather than hinders.[1] Let's look at how to involve professionals at the right time and in the right way.[2]

---

1 Seventy-eight percent of individuals with acute mental illness say they have received psychological therapy to treat their illness. Seventy-nine percent of individuals with acute mental illness who have received psychological therapy believe psychological therapy has been effective (Lifeway Research, *Study of Acute Mental Illness and Christian Faith*, 7, https://research.lifeway.com/wp-content/uploads/2014/09/Acute-Mental-Illness-and-Christian-Faith-Research-Report-1.pdf).

2 Fifty-one percent of pastors, 40 percent of family members, and 25 percent of individuals with acute mental illness believe psychological therapy should be used *after* sharing spiritual principles. Twenty percent of pastors, 18 percent of family members, and 18 percent of individuals with acute mental illness believe psychological therapy should be used *before* sharing spiritual principles. Six percent of pastors, 28 percent of family

There Are Three Main Professional Options in the Short Term

The main professional help categories are:

Primary Care Physician (PCP). If a person is struggling with depression or anxiety but is still able to function in everyday-life activities, the family doctor is usually a good first stop. The PCP will be able to do some basic assessment to determine the nature and severity of the concerns.

The PCP will determine whether this is an illness and how serious it is, usually using standard questionnaires and listening to the story. The doctor will then decide whether he can manage it himself or if he should request a non-urgent referral to specialists. He will provide educational materials, recommend basic medications, and arrange follow-up monitoring of the condition. If the PCP decides that the illness is too severe for non-urgent referral because the sufferer is not able to function in everyday-life activities or is becoming paranoid or delusional, a trip to the urgent care center of the local hospital (medical or psychiatric) is in order.

Emergency Room. Sometimes, though not often, the need is so acute and urgent that a doctor's visit is not possible or practical. That's when the Emergency Room is the best place to go.

Law Enforcement. For those who are a danger to themselves or others and are not willing to see the doctor or visit the ER, a 911 call to seek police help is in order.

---

members, and 34 percent of individuals with acute mental illness believe psychological therapy should be used *without* sharing spiritual principles. Two percent of pastors, family members, and individuals with acute mental illness believe psychological therapy should *never* be used to treat acute mental illness (*Acute Mental Illness and Christian Faith*, 7).

*A serious problem
requires serious professionals.*

How do I decide which approach to pursue first?

The Severity of Illness Determines the First Step

The severity of the sufferer's condition helps us decide whether the first step is the doctor, the ER, or law-enforcement. Some questions to consider in making this decision are:

Is the person a danger to self/others? In more severe forms of depression, bipolar disorder, or schizophrenia, the individual may well be considering harming himself (suicide).

Is the person psychotic (hearing voices, hallucinating, or not in touch with reality)? In mental illnesses such as bipolar disorder, schizoaffective disorder, or schizophrenia, the person may not be able to make sense of reality as he may be hearing voices in his head, sometimes telling him to harm others.

Depending on the level of threat, a trip to the local emergency room or a call to law enforcement may be the first step. A general rule to observe is, "Better to err on the side of caution rather than to wish you had."

*Overreaction can cause difficulties,
underreaction can cause death.*

What kind of treatment can I expect?

There Are Three Levels of Professional Treatment in the Longer Term

Inpatient. This is the highest level of care and involves hospitalization, usually for those who are assessed as a danger to themselves or to others. It is usually required when there are thoughts or plans of suicide, risk-taking behaviors (putting the sufferer or others at risk of harm), or psychosis.

In an inpatient psychiatric hospital unit, sufferers are closely monitored around the clock by a team of trained mental health professionals. Their time and activities through the day are highly structured and focused on immediate stabilization of mood (reduce the intensity of the symptoms) and of functioning in basic life skills (being able to eat, sleep, and interact socially in an appropriate manner). In most cases, inpatient care is short-term. Depending on the level of severity or impairment, it can last from several days to a couple of weeks.

Outpatient. When sufferers are able to care for themselves and are no longer deemed a threat to themselves or others, they are then discharged to outpatient care. In outpatient care, they would be living independently or with a family member but continuing to receive services for long-term stabilization of the mental illness. The frequency of the care in outpatient care (daily, weekly, or monthly) is determined on the basis of how much assistance the sufferers need to maintain and build stability in their everyday functioning. In other words, the higher the level of functioning and the lower the intensity of symptoms, the less frequent the need for appointments with the treatment provider.

In both inpatient and outpatient care, there are two main types of professionals who administer the bulk of the sufferer's care. The psychiatric provider (doctor, nurse practitioner, or physician's assistant) evaluates and prescribes medications for mood stabilization. The counselor (PhD- or Masters-level psychologist or social worker) provides talk therapy to assist the person in better understanding and coping with the illness.

Both the psychiatric provider and the counselor may offer individual counseling (meeting alone with the sufferer), family counseling (meeting with the sufferer and family), or group therapy (meeting with several sufferers at once). The treatment providers communicate with each other to coordinate care and to monitor or measure progress in the treatment. Each of these professionals lends a different aspect of expertise to assist in the treatment process, and one should not be neglected at the expense of the other. The psychiatric provider's medications assist in correcting imbalance of brain chemicals; the counseling provides skills and insights to better cope with the illness.

Primary Care Provider. With mild to moderate mental illness, a PCP can arrange for counseling and psychiatry services, although both can take longer to access.

When choosing professional mental health care, we should take the same care we would in choosing any medical professional. We may not have much choice when in the emergency room for a few hours. However, on an outpatient basis we do have more ability to research and choose a professional who best matches our need and shares similar values. Some questions to ask when trying to select a counselor are:

- Does the therapist possess and manifest a personal and growing relationship with Jesus Christ?
- Does the therapist possess and demonstrate a genuine love and concern for people who are hurting?

- Does the therapist base her work on a biblical worldview and value system?
- Is the therapist willing to work with the person's pastor, keeping him informed and involved in accordance with the patient's information release forms?
- Will the appropriate release forms be made available to maintain a healthy confidentiality boundary?
- Does the therapist have the appropriate professional training, credentials, experience, and state licensure as a certified mental health professional?

If we do refer, though, it is vital to maintain regular contact with the sufferer so that he does not feel discarded or forgotten.

---

*God provides care for us
by providing caregivers for us.*

SUMMARY

Problem: Neither family and friends nor the church can manage the illness on their own.

Insights: (1) There are three professional options. (2) The severity of the problem determines the first step. (3) There are three levels of professional treatment.

Action: Access the right level of professional support at the right time for the right treatment.

- Ask primary care providers, ER workers, inpatient and outpatient staff and to share their stories of dealing with various kinds of mental illness.
- Pray for such professional caregivers, and thank God for his care through them.
- Get to know Christians in each of these categories and use them as a resource where possible.
- Determine what questions to ask to ensure that you find the professional help that is most consistent with the Bible.

Tom's Story about Cheryl

In early adulthood, Cheryl began to be withdrawn and isolated (story continued from chapter 14). She was afraid to venture out of the house. She stopped wearing her nice clothes, fixing her hair, and using makeup, and even showering. When she stopped eating, her roommates contacted her family. By the time her family was able to get her to agree to help, she was despairing of life itself and she was referred to inpatient psychiatric hospitalization. She was eventually able to be stabilized with a combination of counseling and psychiatric medications.

She maintained a close connection with her mental health providers for many years and remained mostly stable. However, after her psychiatrist retired and her counselor moved to a different city, she dropped out of mental health treatment. Eventually her mood became more unstable and her thoughts became confused and paranoid.

When Craig and Brad became involved, she agreed to discuss her illness with her family doctor (PCP). Her doctor was able to get her started with a mild dose of mood stabilizing medication before referring her to a psychiatrist, who prescribed a combination of medications tailored to address her unique blend of symptoms. Her PCP was also able to connect her with a Christian counselor to assist her in understanding and accepting her mental illness, in developing and practicing coping strategies, and in making the best use of the support offered by her biological and church family.

16

What Role Does Medication Have?

ONE OF THE HARDEST QUESTIONS is whether medication should be part of the treatment of mental illness. There are many confusing and contradictory answers to this question.

Some say, "Never!" They rule them out in all circumstances as spiritually and physically dangerous. Others say, "Take meds and take them immediately." However, that may hinder deeper consideration of what might have caused or contributed to the mental illness. It may also prevent the discovery of what might be the benefit of waiting, what might be the side-effects, or what other measures should be taken in addition to meds.

We want to suggest three principles to inform and guide decisions regarding medications.

We Don't Run to Them First

Our culture is suffering from an over-prescription of medications, with meds for mental illness being some of the most overused.[1] This is partly because of today's "instant cure" culture. We are not

---

1 "Ninety-four percent of individuals with acute mental illness say they have been prescribed medication to treat their mental illness" (Lifeway Research, *Study of Acute Mental Illness and*

willing to suffer anything for even a brief time without seeking some alleviation of the pain and discomfort by means of medication. This is especially true when it comes to sadness, anxiety, confusion, and other emotional and mental challenges. If there's a pill, we take it and ask no further questions. There's no attempt made to address other physical or spiritual issues. There's no seeking of God's help, grace, and counsel. "Just give me something to make me feel better!"

One of the results of this rush to medications is that people miss out on the opportunity for spiritual healing and spiritual growth from affliction. We medicate away guilt, shame, fear, and confusion, without asking deeper questions. We want quick healing and therefore short-circuit the spiritual fruit that grows only in the soil of patience in suffering. There's also little weighing of the potential side-effects of medication.

> *We look to doctors for a cheap prescription
> rather than looking to God for
> priceless sanctification.*

So, are we saying, "Never go on meds for mental illness"? No, not at all. We're simply saying that unless the situation is already dangerous or desperately bad, medications shouldn't be the first option we consider. But we mustn't rush to the other extreme of ruling them out altogether.

Christian Faith, 6, https://research.lifeway.com/wp-content/uploads/2014/09/Acute-Mental -Illness-and-Christian-Faith-Research-Report-1.pdf).

We Don't Rule Them Out Altogether

When we see people going to one extreme on an issue, there's always the danger that we'll rush to the other extreme. That's happened with meds for mental illness, especially with anti-depressants and antianxiety drugs. Some have seen the overuse and abuse of these meds and have said, "The only safe response is to rule them out."[2]

Others rule out meds because they don't know or understand the role of the brain in our thinking and feeling processes, and therefore its role in our spiritual lives. If the brain is part of the machinery that processes our perceptions, thoughts, and feelings, and, like every other organ, has been damaged by the fall, we can expect it to break at times. Like the factory with a broken conveyor belt, it doesn't matter how many high-quality raw materials you put into it, the goods are going to come out damaged until the machinery is fixed. The denial of mental disorders or of the possibility that meds could help is essentially a denial of biblical anthropology in that it is a denial of the extensive, damaging effects of the fall upon our whole humanity.

Pride may be another reason why some people rule out meds. We don't want to think of ourselves as weak (and we certainly don't want others to think of us in that way). Strange, isn't it, that no one would view taking medication for any other malfunctioning bodily organ as a sign of weakness? Rather, that's wisdom! Yet,

2   The extreme nature of this position was highlighted in our research, which found that, while "0 percent of pastors, 0 percent of family members, and only 1 percent of individuals with acute mental illness believe medications should never be used to treat acute mental illness" (*Acute Mental Illness and Christian Faith*, 7), the reluctance to consider medications can be seen in the fact that 7 percent of pastors, 12 percent of family members, and 7 percent of individuals with acute mental illness say medications should be used only as a last resort (*Acute Mental Illness and Christian Faith*, 24).

taking meds for problems with the most complex organ in the body is somehow only for "losers"!

Another reason that meds are refused is a false spirituality. Although Christians with heart disease, diabetes, blood disorders, or cancer do not think that it is unspiritual to seek and use medicines to relieve their symptoms and even cure their illness, many seem to think that there is some special spiritual virtue in suffering mental illness for months and years without any medical intervention. Family and friends, however, don't usually see much virtue in this approach! Taking meds can be an act of self-denial and of service to others.

Others might say they're afraid of the side-effects. The side-effects of antidepressants are often overplayed by those who oppose any medical contribution to the treatment of depression. And it's often used as an excuse by those who are resistant to taking them. However, we must accept that, as with all meds, there will sometimes be some side-effects to taking meds for mental illness. Again, it's strange to see the way that we will put up with some quite serious side-effects when it comes to the treatment of strokes, angina, or cancer, and yet, with meds for mental illness we seem to demand perfect results with zero side-effects. The question really is, "How desperate are we?" If we are truly desperate, then we will be prepared to put up with some lesser side-effects in order to start feeling and thinking normally again.

Whatever the reason for ruling out meds, it often makes things worse in the long run. The sufferer continues to suffer, usually they will get worse, the delay is actually weakening their bones and other vital organs,[3] and the family and friends suffer the consequences

---

3   Once again, we recommend the following article, which summarizes and links to recent scientific research: David Murray, "Can Depression Be Cured? Recent Research," October 16, 2016, https://headhearthand.org/blog/2016/10/14/can-depression-be-cured-latest-research/.

too. With 85 percent of individuals who have been prescribed medication for acute mental illness believing that their medication has been effective, we are losing a lot of potential healing if we rule out medications altogether.[4]

When we refuse to consider meds,
we are refusing to consider our family.

"If I take meds, is that all I have to do?"
No, they must be taken as part of a holistic package of care.

We Don't Rely on Them Alone

It's extremely rare for mental illness medications to work without a serious commitment to receiving and acting upon counsel about lifestyle, decision-making, social interaction, and spiritual needs. If someone thinks that the sole answer to mental illness is a pill, they are in for a very long and dark journey. However, when medications are taken as part of a holistic package of care for the body, mind, and soul, they can be highly effective.

If the mental illness is especially serious, sometimes these other measures may need to wait. Time may be needed for the medications to have an affect so that rationality returns and counseling can be received, processed, and acted upon. Medications often enable other areas of treatment to be successfully addressed. They are like

---

4 Lifeway Research, *Acute Mental Illness and Christian Faith*, 6. And that's not just imaginary. Seventy-eight percent of family members in a household of someone with acute mental illness said medication has been effective (*Acute Mental Illness and Christian Faith*, 7).

the ladder thrown down into the pit which enables the sufferer to at least begin to climb out.

Meds alone will rarely cure
but meds enable and multiply other cures.

SUMMARY

Problem: Medications can be overused, underused, or misused.

Insights: When it comes to medications, (1) we don't run to them first, (2) we don't rule them out altogether, and (3) we don't rely on them alone.

Action: Take professional and pastoral advice on the role of medications in the treatment of mental illness so that the right meds are used for the right person at the right time and in the right way.

- Ask medical professionals and pastoral counselors for their input and pray that God would guide them in their directions.
- Thank God for medications as one of his gifts and blessings rather than despising or refusing them.
- Ensure that medications are only part of a balanced holistic package of spiritual, physical, mental, and social measures.

David's Story

I've often seen Christians break the three "rules" in this chapter, causing damage and sometimes disasters. But I've also seen Christians prayerfully and patiently work through the process, taking both medical and spiritual advice. They've then humbly accepted God's gift of medications with gratitude and used them along with other measures to move toward healing, or, at least, to better management of their sickness and suffering.

However, I have to confess that, even though I'd had a lot of experience with this and saw God's good gift of meds used well and helping many, I was still reluctant to accept my own need for medication. I fell into the second error of proud and stubborn refusal of meds, even though the many other steps I was taking were not improving my situation. Eventually, Shona pleaded with me to at least have a doctor evaluate me. It was then I realized how great my need was, and how much I needed meds to make all the other measures work.

17

What Role Do Biblical Counselors Have?

HAVING CONSIDERED the roles of pastors, the church family, family and friends, mental health professionals, and medication in the treatment of mental illness, we want now to think about the role of biblical counselors. We've noticed that there is often a gap between mental health professionals on one side and pastors on the other side. Mental health professionals have so much more experience, expertise, and time, that it can be tempting for the pastor just to hand over all care to the professional. However, sufferers and those who care for them also need spiritual support and direction as well as protection from unbiblical counsel. That's where *biblical* counselors come in and can be so helpful.

Biblical Counselors Help with Spiritual Issues

God did not design the Bible to be a medical textbook. Just as we don't turn to the Bible for detailed guidance on a healthy diet, so we shouldn't expect the Bible to provide detailed guidance on mental health. However, God did design the Bible to be a sufficient guide for the spiritual dimensions of all issues. Biblical counsel is therefore a vital part of any package of care for sufferers. That's where biblical counselors come in. These counselors usually don't have professional mental health qualifications or training. However, they will usually have some specialized theological training and experience in counseling from the Bible. So, with what spiritual aspects of care can they help?

First, they help to discern any spiritual causes behind mental illness. As we've previously discussed, sin can be the cause of some mental illness, and biblical counselors are experts in helping sufferers identify these sins and helping them repent of them and put on new patterns of obedience. They will often give homework that will help the sufferer and will hold them accountable at their regular meetings. If the cause is spiritual and the depression is mild to moderate, often biblical counseling is all that a sufferer needs.

Second, even if there is no spiritual cause to the mental illness, there are always spiritual consequences such as confusion, fear, sadness, coldness, backsliding, withdrawal from church, and so on. Biblical counselors can help sufferers with these internal and external consequences.

Third, biblical counselors can offer sufferers spiritual support as they continue to receive treatment from mental health professionals who deal with other dimensions of the problem. They can sustain them spiritually with regular prayer, worship, and Bible study.

Spiritual issues may not be central,
but they are never peripheral.

How does the biblical counselor relate to others involved in caring?

Biblical Counselors Bridge the Gaps

With something as complicated as mental illness, it's almost inevitable that relational problems will arise and will have to be dealt with. A biblical counselor can have an important role here in bridging these gaps and reconciling these relationships.

For example, there can be tension between sufferers and their family and friends (and their church and employer). Many misunderstandings and sinful frustrations can develop, straining this important connection. Biblical counselors are often well trained in Christian reconciliation. They can also help bridge the gap between the sufferer and the church. Where there's been withdrawal and isolation, biblical counselors can help sufferers ease back into the life of the church and reconnect.

But the most important bridge-building role that biblical counselors can play is standing in the gap between the pastor/church and mental health professionals. The biblical counselor has the gifts and time to communicate information between the parties and ensure that the professionals are doing what they can without straying into spiritual and pastoral issues, and vice versa. The biblical counselor is able to identify any dangerous counsel or direction the sufferer is receiving from the professionals and protect the sufferer from it.

The biblical counselor also bridges the gap between sufferers and their church family. Biblical counselors usually place a high priority on the local church and therefore want to embed sufferers and their care of them in the local church.

Mental illness opens gaps,
biblical counseling stands in them.

What about the long term? Is the biblical counselor just a short-term fix?

Biblical Counselors Build Long-Term Relationships

Few pastors have the time needed to build close spiritual relationships with sufferers. As we said earlier, elders can take on more on this front. However, they often lack expertise in this area. A biblical counselor can be of special help because he or she can combine the relational with the spiritual and therefore be a long-term blessing to sufferers.

They can also build confidence in the mental health professionals who are willing to work with the person's faith rather than against it. And if they find out that the opposite is happening, they can guide the sufferer away from this danger to safer counsel. Biblical counselors often have contacts in the mental health field and can give reliable recommendations of those who will work with the church and the counselor rather than against them.

Biblical counseling
is relational counseling.

SUMMARY

Problem: Christian experts are needed to deal with the spiritual causes and consequences of depression, bridge gaps in care for sufferers, and protect sufferers from unbiblical and harmful counsel.

Insights: Biblical counselors (1) help with spiritual issues, (2) bridge the gaps, and (3) build long-term relationships.

Action: Use biblical counselors to assist healing in the spiritual realm and to stand in the gaps that can result from mental illness.

- Get to know biblical counselors in your area.
- Find out what their biblical views are and whether they use a holistic approach to mental illness.
- Ensure that sufferers and those who care for them get good, regular biblical counseling.

David's Story

I first discovered biblical counseling at seminary in the 1990s. In my youthful zeal and ignorance, I thought it was the answer to everyone's problems, including mental health problems. Through books and lectures, the early biblical counseling movement persuaded me that doctors, psychiatrists, and psychologists had no place in dealing with things like depression, schizophrenia, and so on—that it was almost always sin issues, and therefore only pastors or biblical counselors had any role in caring.

However, as I experienced more of life, met more mental health professionals, and came to understand the Bible better, I realized that while biblical counseling has an important role in the care of those with mental illness, it is not an exclusive role. Along with others in the biblical counseling movement, I have worked to bring biblical counseling to a balanced and more biblical approach to mental illness.

Thirty years on, most biblical counselors today are more inclusive and holistic than the early biblical counseling pioneers. They still have an important role in any Christian approach to mental illness, but also recognize their limitations and the importance of building a holistic team approach to mental and emotional problems.

18

What Role Does the Sufferer Have?

SOMETIMES SUFFERERS can take on a passive, victim spirit when suffering with mental illness. So much care can be provided by their pastor, church, family, friends, professionals, and biblical counselors that they can begin to simply be receivers of care rather than taking any responsibility for their own recovery. This diminishing of personal responsibility is harmful to the sufferer and prolongs the suffering. We want to encourage sufferers to do what they can without heaping false guilt upon them by blaming them for what is outside of their control.

The Sufferer's Role Will Vary

There are a number of factors that we have to weigh when considering what to expect of sufferers. First, there are different illnesses. Obviously, we will have different expectations of someone with schizophrenia or psychosis than of those with anxiety.

Second, there are different levels of severity. All mental illnesses are on a scale, with some being mild and others being severe, and everything in between. For example, someone with a severe anxiety disorder will have less responsibility than someone with episodes of mild anxiety.

Third, there are different stages of recovery. We will be more patient and tolerant with someone just beginning to climb out of the pit than with someone who has been on the mend for many months.

Fourth, there are different levels of support. We will expect more of someone who has a strong home base and family/church support than someone who is homeless and lacking any social connections.

The sufferer can't do everything
but can do something.

Is there really that much that sufferers can do? As previously mentioned, that will vary depending on a number of factors. But their role is vital.

The Sufferer's Role Is Vital

What should we say to sufferers in general about their responsibility in this area? First, we should encourage them to submit to external advice even if it contradicts their own feelings and thoughts. They have to learn to trust others at times like these, because they are not trustworthy analysts of their own state or of what will help them. Trusting those outside of themselves is a way of trusting the God who put these caregivers in their lives. That also means doing the homework counselors give them, even if they feel it is pointless.

Second, they must comply with medication. Noncompliance with medication is one of the main reasons why people take much longer to recover, or why they think their medication is not working. Instead of letting them rely on their own memories, arrange a box with the days marked on it and make sure the pills are taken at the right time and in the right doses.

Third, we urge them to do the basics. Insofar as they can, we want them to work hard at regular and healthy sleep, diet, and exercise. We want them to keep to the same daily routine and timing each day, ensure that daily spiritual disciplines are present, and that they are in church on Sunday.

The suffering won't let up
until the sufferer steps up.

What benefits are there in the sufferer stepping up?

The Sufferer's Role Gives Value

Although the responsibilities mentioned above may not seem like a lot, they can make a massive difference. First, it benefits the sufferer with a sense of purpose. A passive victim has no self-esteem, no self-worth. Calling people to responsibility gives them a sense of moral agency and inherent dignity. They are active participants and not just passive observers. They have a reason to live. They have a purpose to perform.

As long as this is kept within reasonable bounds and expectations, sufferers taking personal responsibility wherever they can will ultimately shorten their suffering. They will get better quicker as they use all the means God has provided.

The end result of this is that everyone benefits—the sufferer and the caregivers, both inside and outside the church family.

Passivity diminishes value,
activity increases value.

SUMMARY

Problem: Sufferers can be absolved of too much personal responsibility or else can have too much heaped upon them, both of which increase the suffering and recovery time.

Insights: The sufferer's role (1) will vary, (2) is vital, and (3) gives value.

Action: Encourage the sufferer to take appropriate levels of responsibility so that they can gain a sense of purpose and shorten recovery.

- Set realistic targets for the sufferer in the areas of sleep, exercise, diet, and spiritual disciplines, and keep them accountable.
- Ask the sufferer what you can do to help her with the things she needs to do.
- Encourage the sufferer to compare how she feels when she takes responsibility compared to when she excuses herself.

Tom's Story

The hardest part of dealing with a mental illness is denial ("This isn't happening to me"). The next most difficult part is minimizing ("This is not a big deal"). The alternative, that makes treatment and positive change possible, is simply admitting, "This is real and this is happening to me."

The first step in the healing process is acceptance of and admitting, "I have a problem." The second step is ownership of the fact that "I have an active role in my treatment." In other words, seeking and showing up for treatment is not all there is to getting better. I have to do the work necessary in order for healing to be experienced.

For years, I had assisted others with acceptance of their illness; however, when it came to myself, I completely missed it! I tried to explain my struggles as "Not a big deal," and, "It's just a slump I'm going through, and it will soon pass." It wasn't until Ruthanne insisted, "You need to be honest with yourself and me," that I could face reality for what it was: I was a helper but I needed help. It was a relief, and I was able to reach out for the help I needed.

19

How Can We Discern Faith and Spiritual Fruit in a Sufferer?

HOW CAN I KNOW if my loved one is a Christian or not?[1] When we see the impact of mental illness on a loved one, especially the spiritual inconsistency and unpredictability, that question can cause much perplexity and sleepless nights. It's easy to see the "growth" in sinful words and actions; it's more difficult to discern graces and fruits of the Spirit in a sufferer.[2] It's easy to see weakness; it's hard to see strength. The sufferers themselves may lose assurance, and we may lose assurance about their faith. Or the sufferers may simply "forget to tell a mental health provider about struggles with their faith because they are more focused on the surface issues of the illness."[3]

---

1   Regarding the eternal salvation of those individuals in a state of psychosis, 45 percent of pastors believe that "Scripture does not say what will happen to those in a state of psychosis, so we cannot say" (Lifeway Research, *Study of Acute Mental Illness and Christian Faith*, 6, https://research.lifeway.com/wp-content/uploads/2014/09/Acute-Mental-Illness-and-Christian-Faith-Research-Report-1.pdf).

2   Mental health experts told Lifeway that we must "be realistic about how much spiritual growth or progress is to be expected of loved ones dealing with mental illness" (*Acute Mental Illness and Christian Faith*, 5).

3   *Acute Mental Illness and Christian Faith*, 5.

On the other hand, "people who deal with mental illness tend to be more honest about their relationship with God."[4]

Despite such difficulties, God has provided some markers to help us navigate to a true and safe answer in assessing the state of a person's faith.[5]

Discerning Faith and Fruit Is an Important Christian Duty

God calls us to self-examination and other-examination when discerning whether faith is present, and what fruits of the Spirit are in evidence.

Self-examination. The Bible instructs us to examine ourselves as to whether we are "in the faith" (2 Cor. 13:5; see also 2 Pet. 1:10–11; Phil. 2:12) and whether there is any fruit in our lives (Gal. 5:22–24). This is a duty that all Christians are called to. It is so important to get a right answer to this question, and we do so by comparing the word of God with our lives, an exercise that involves faith and reason.

Other-examination. The Bible also calls us to other-examination. Though we have to be careful not to assume God's place, who alone can decide whether a person is a believer or not, we are to provisionally discern a person's heart from the fruit they produce in their lives (Matt. 7:15–20).

---

*Faith examination is done
by fruit examination.*

---

4 *Acute Mental Illness and Christian Faith*, 5.
5 Longer discussion of this question can be found in the supplementary research study, "Discerning Faith and Its Fruits in Mental Illness," forthcoming.

We accept that the Bible calls God's people to self-examination and other-examination, but does that apply to people with mental illness?

There Are Many Additional Challenges with Mental Illness

While the question of whether a person has fruit or faith is a difficult question at the best of times, it's doubly hard in a person with mental illness. There are additional complications to deal with.

Illness makes it hard to judge. Illness is never a good time to judge anyone's spiritual state. Think of how holy or spiritual you felt the last time you had a bad cold or the flu. That's even more so when it's mental illness. During such times, sanctification can halt or even reverse in the heart and life of the believer. Dealing with the intensity of the pain uses up all the person's physical and mental energy. Or there's the problem that "some manic episodes can appear to be signs of devotion or sacrifice."[6] For example, a Christian may give away all their money and many of their possessions during a manic episode. Or they may stay up all night praying or witnessing online.

Mental illness makes it even harder to judge. All of us struggle to one degree or another with unstable thoughts and emotions, which influence our judgment of where we're at spiritually. This can put us on an emotional roller-coaster, especially when we put our trust in the feelings of the moment (good or bad, happy or sad, victorious or defeated), leading to instability and sometimes despair.[7]

As mental illness, by definition, affects the thoughts and the emotions, depressing them or sending them into uncontrollable

---

6 Lifeway Research, *Acute Mental Illness and Christian Faith*, 5.

7 Lifeway reported that mental health experts said, "In most cases, the illness needs to be stabilized before spiritual growth will take place" (*Acute Mental Illness and Christian Faith*, 5).

ups and downs, reasoning like Einstein one moment then totally irrational the next, it is especially difficult to judge a person's spiritual state in these times. One minute we're rejoicing at the faith of our loved one, and the next we're despairing at their unbelief and sinfulness. One moment their faith is so real, the next they are detached from reality, or worse, wallowing in fleshly practices. One day they are able to reason their way to faith, another day, in a state of psychosis, they seem to have no reason *or* faith. How can we have any certainty and get any comfort? How do we discern between weakness and sin?

Faith and fruit are hard to see
when thoughts and feelings are all at sea.

So, is discerning faith and fruits an impossible task when someone has mental illness? Are there any truths to help me in this?

There Are Truths to Comfort the Heart

When what we're seeing and hearing in the daily life of a sufferer is so discouraging, we can turn to God's never-changing, ever-reliable word and encourage ourselves with three aspects of God's character.[8]

God's sovereignty (Jonah 2:9). Salvation is God's work from before time began until time is no more and everything in between (Rom.

---

8 "Thirty-nine percent of individuals with acute mental illness agree that their local church has specifically helped them think through and live out their faith in the context of their mental illness. Among individuals with acute mental illness who attended church regularly as an adult, 57 percent agree that their local church has specifically helped them think through and live out their faith in the context of their mental illness" (*Acute Mental Illness and Christian Faith*, 8).

8:28–29). This means that salvation is God's work, not ours or anyone else's, and therefore it is not dependent on a person's work or even their sanity. God can preserve a person's faith even when we cannot or they cannot. He can give a person with mental illness more faith than those who have full control of their faculties. This is where a strong view of God's sovereignty in salvation can give more hope than some theological views that major on functioning human reason and "free will."

God's faithfulness (Phil. 1:6). Even when we prove unfaithful, God is faithful. He loyally sticks with us. If we are his, he will never give us up. God has given us promises of his faithfulness that we can rely on.

We start many projects that we never finish. God never does that. He does not start a work only to scrap or discard it. He doesn't neglect or forget his work. When he begins a work of grace, he will complete it. He finishes what he starts. If God has begun a work, even many years before, and years of faithfulness preceded this illness, don't doubt in the dark what God has revealed in the light.[9]

God's mercy. One of the ways God demonstrates that salvation is by his mercy and grace is in saving those who could not save themselves. We think of babies who miscarried or were aborted in the womb. We think of children who died before reaching

---

9   As will be mentioned in chapter 23, we borrow this thought from V. Raymond Edman, *The Disciplines of Life* (Wheaton, IL: Van Kampen, 1948). "Fifty-four percent of pastors, 57 percent of family members, and 40 percent of individuals with acute mental illness strongly agree that someone who is initiated into the Christian faith and church and later experiences acute mental illness that keeps them from living like a Christian will still receive eternal salvation" (*Acute Mental Illness and Christian Faith*, 6). Doctrinal considerations enter the discussion here, because Christians who believe in the perseverance of the saints do not believe that a true believer can ever be lost, whereas some Christians believe the opposite.

the age of accountability. We think of those with cognitive disabilities. None of these had the ability to hear and believe the gospel. Yet, Christians have always believed that God may, and most likely will, save a large number if not all of them, to show that he is a merciful God who saves by grace alone. Could it be that Christians with mental illness fall into a related category? Although they are unable mentally to process truth and respond rightly to it, God does not give them up but rather shows again so clearly that he saves not according to a person's abilities but according to his mercy.

Similar spiritual questions are raised by the challenge of mental disabilities. For example, what degree of mental disability diminishes a person's spiritual responsibility? This question is complicated of course by the different ages at which mental illness begins to be suffered. For example, some may become mentally ill before the age of accountability; for others it may be after the age of accountability but before a person is regenerated by the Spirit; for still others it may come on after the age of accountability and after being regenerated by the Spirit.

God's character comforts us
when Christian character doesn't.

SUMMARY

Problem: It is difficult (for both sufferers and caregivers) to discern faith and fruits of the Spirit in a sufferer.

Insights: (1) Discerning grace and fruit is an important Christian duty. (2) There are many additional challenges with mental illness. (3) There are precious truths to comfort the heart.

Action: Discern faith and fruit in the mentally ill, while remaining aware of both the special challenges and the comforting truths.

- Consider the ways illness has affected faith and fruit in your own life and the lives of others.
- Think of the evident fruits of faith in your life or a loved one's life before mental illness.
- Highlight spiritual fruits that remain in sufferer's lives, even if fewer and smaller.
- Bring God's character to sufferers to encourage their faith.

David's Story

My first real challenge with mental illness came when Shona plunged into a severe depression around the birth of our fourth child. As her depression manifested itself largely in her spiritual life, it was easy to conclude that she had a spiritual problem. She had such awful thoughts of God and felt so spiritually dead that she decided she was not a Christian. What I eventually learned was the importance of helping Shona focus on objective facts rather than subjective feelings. Although she had no positive spiritual feelings and sometimes had terrible spiritual feelings, I helped her see

objective spiritual fruits in her life from the past and even
in the present.

I also saw the importance of redirecting her reading, listening, and thinking to objective truths about God rather than
what she felt about God. When she brought God's character
and historical acts into view, that did bring her peace in a
way that searching for feelings of love, faith, and hope in
her heart did not. This comforted her and encouraged her
that she was still a believer. Instead of trying to read whole
chapters with an exhausted mind and getting nothing, she
started reading just one verse a day, and her limited resources
were able to process that and give her spiritual hope as well
until she was able gradually to increase her reading back to
her normal reading schedule.

20

How Can We Help a Sufferer Grow Spiritually?

LET'S ASSUME THAT, despite the difficulties in discerning faith and fruit in the mentally ill, we are encouraged that spiritual life does exist. The next question should be, how can we help this believer grow spiritually? Although most sufferers believe they can still thrive spiritually, as do their families,[1] there are still one in five sufferers who think spiritual growth and mental illness are incompatible.[2]

Again, as with discerning faith and fruit, we are up against multiple difficulties with mental illness: intensified emotions, increased

---

1   Seventy-six percent of pastors agree that a Christian with an acute mental illness can thrive spiritually regardless of whether or not the illness has been stabilized. Seventy-three percent of individuals with acute mental illness and 74 percent of family members in a household of someone with acute mental illness agree that a Christian with an acute mental illness can thrive spiritually even if the illness has not been stabilized. Eighty-eight percent of individuals with acute mental illness and 95 percent of family members in a household of someone with acute mental illness agree that a Christian with an acute mental illness can thrive spiritually after the illness has been stabilized (Lifeway Research, *Study of Acute Mental Illness and Christian Faith*, 6, https://research.lifeway.com/wp-content/uploads/2014/09/Acute-Mental-Illness-and-Christian-Faith-Research-Report-1.pdf).

2   *Serving Those with Mental Illness* (Colorado Springs: Focus on the Family, 2014), 6, https://media.focusonthefamily.com/pastoral/pdf/PAS_eBook_Series_Mental_Health_INTERACTIVE.pdf. Twenty-eight percent of individuals with acute mental illness agree their mental illness hurt/hurts their ability to live like a Christian (*Acute Mental Illness and Christian Faith*, 6).

emotional pain, accelerated thoughts, inability to concentrate. There's no question that, just as faith is hard when someone is mentally ill, so is spiritual growth. So, what can we do to overcome the challenges and advance spiritual growth?

Physical Presence Is Best

When ministering to such sufferers, we want to do many of the same basic things we would do with anyone going through difficult life circumstances and providences. While text messages and calls are good, physical presence is much better. Just being there, even if not talking, is therapeutic company for the sufferer.

Physical presence is made even more powerful when you are present emotionally too. Within appropriate contexts and with suitable safeguards, warmth, kindness, hugs, physical touch, all play important roles, even more so than in ordinary life. Express your care and concern with eye-contact, facial expressions, body language, and gentle words.

In terms of when to meet, the ideal is for a regular time to be set for getting together so that it becomes a fixed regular event in the calendar rather than trying to arrange this each week with all the unpredictability that involves. Also, ask them when they are at their best in the day. For some it's the morning, for others the afternoon. If the person doesn't agree to regular meetings, then try to phone before visiting. If they're not picking up the phone, just show up at times when you know they are at home and unoccupied.

---

*Our physical presence
can bring God's presence.*

So, I'm with the person, what do I do now?

A Proper Spiritual Attitude Is Necessary

We want to approach this meeting with a Christlike spirit, which would include the following:

Be silent. Remember when Job's friends came to be with him and spent seven days in silence? That was their most effective treatment, far more so than when they began to open their mouths! Quiet times are okay times, though probably seven days is rather long in most circumstances!

Be patient. Even when you are not able to minister and encourage for long, even when meetings and visits are cut short, or conversation and responsiveness is minimal, don't give up. Persevere, wait a while, return, do and say what you can, and trust the Lord to multiply your "few loaves and fishes."

Be kind. This is an opportunity to show Christ's gentleness and compassion. How would Jesus interact with this person?

Be prayerful. Pray before you go. Pray with them. Pray afterwards. Encourage the person to say prayers after you, or even to stumble through a prayer of his own.

Be truthful. By this we mean, be full of truth in your ministry to sufferers. Ask them for Bible passages they want to be read. Read aloud to them, inviting them to join in reading or to read themselves. Perhaps read daily devotionals that are bright and inspirational. Even if they can comprehend only at a basic level, God can bless his word. King Nebuchadnezzar experienced mental illness at the hand of God but was still able to repent of his sins, regain his mental faculties, and praise the Lord for how God had struck him (Dan. 4:28–37).

Be an encourager. Don't go to be a critic. Highlight any good in their lives, affirm it, and delight in it. Be bright and hopeful without being too high-energy.

Be God-centered. Focus on truths that are objective and true regardless of what the person feels or thinks. Focus on things such as God's character, Christ's person and work, the atonement, justification, adoption, salvation by grace, or heaven.

> *Objective truth is a cure*
> *for subjective trouble.*

So, does growth just happen then, or should we have a strategy?

Spiritual Progress Is Possible

If we follow the above guidelines, and the illness is relatively stable, then spiritual progress is possible. Here are some areas to focus on when you're trying to help a person grow, even amid mental illness.

Progress in prayer. It is often helpful to have sufferers write out a prayer and then speak it out loud. Or provide written prayers for them to read. Routine and regularity are key. Better frequent and small than rare and long.

Progress in Bible reading. Start with a verse a day of Bible reading. Then add another a few days later, and so on. Again, better small and focused than long and distracted. Ask them to write down one lesson from what they read.

Progress in worship. Spending time in God's presence, even when it's not felt, is beneficial. Use psalms, hymns, and spiritual songs

(Eph. 5:19) to deepen and lengthen worship. Listen to worship songs and sing along with them.

Progress in submission. In the case of suffering, often the greatest area of growth will be in submission to God, accepting the illness rather than fighting God over it. Even if the illness remains constant or perhaps even gets worse, submitting to it can be an area of growth.

Progress in fruit. Highlight one fruit of the Spirit which is still visible and try to work on it, cultivate it, water it, fertilize it, and so on. If fruit is growing anywhere in the garden, that's encouraging.

Progress in gifts. Find out what spiritual gifts a person exercised before the illness, and find a way for that gift to be exercised today, though perhaps not so publicly or regularly. Illness does not necessarily mean that all opportunities to serve cease to exist. While sufferers can't do everything, most can do more than nothing.

One of the most encouraging verses for the mentally ill is, "Likewise the Spirit helps us in our weakness. For we do not know what to pray for as we ought, but the Spirit himself intercedes for us with groanings too deep for words. And he who searches hearts knows what is the mind of the Spirit, because the Spirit intercedes for the saints according to the will of God" (Rom. 8:26–27). As Eric Johnson put it, "The Spirit would seem to lie 'beneath' our consciousness and takes our inarticulate longings to the Father, shaping them according to his will."[3] How encouraging for those who have groans instead of reason!

Sufferers also can experience Christ's strength being made perfect in their weakness in ways that the strong and healthy cannot. They can know Christ's sympathy for their weakness in a wonderful way (Heb. 4:15).

---

3 Eric L. Johnson, *Foundations for Soul Care* (Downers Grove, IL: IVP Academic, 2007), 407.

Suffering stops some growth
but starts other growth.

SUMMARY

Problem: Spiritual growth is very difficult in mental illness.

Insights: (1) Physical presence is best. (2) A proper spiritual attitude is necessary. (3) Spiritual progress is possible.

Action: Help sufferers to grow spiritually by physical presence, a proper spiritual approach, and God's means of grace. A number of practical action points are already included in this article. Choose one at a time and focus on growth in one area at a time.

David's Story

A lot of the Christians I've counseled regarding depression or anxiety have been Type-A hyperachievers who have burned out. They are used to getting lots done in short times. Whether it's work, sports, education, or friendships, they want to go fast and far, and they have, thus far.

That's why mental illness is so painful for these kinds of personalities (I include myself in this). But it's also probably why God brings mental illness into our lives—to slow us down and make us more dependent on him than on ourselves. That doesn't feel like spiritual growth, but it's often where God wants to grow us.

Whenever we are caring for someone with mental illness, we don't want to say, "Well, Christian growth doesn't matter right now." Neither do we want to say, "You should be so much stronger spiritually." Rather, we want to help them accept "small" and "slow." Practice makes progress. Growth does not mean perfection but progression. One of the skills we need to develop is looking for new metrics of new kinds of growth.

21

How Can We Help Sufferers Serve in the Church?

SUFFERERS TEND TO miss out or pass on serving opportunities in the church. They are left out by others who do not expect them to serve while experiencing mental illness. They pass up opportunities because they think that it is beyond them or that they'd make a mess of it, or they can't recognize their gifts. Most often the self-focus that accompanies mental illness blocks thinking about serving others.

So how do we help the sufferer serve in the church? It looks hopelessly difficult, but it isn't. There's much that can be done. Let's see what we can do to help.

Every Christian Serves God and His Church

Whether we are young or old, male or female, educated or uneducated, popular or unknown, rich or poor, healthy or unhealthy, the apostle Peter exhorts Christians to "proclaim the excellencies of him who called you out of darkness into his marvelous light" (1 Pet. 2:9).

In Romans 12:1, the apostle Paul addresses all Christians: "I appeal to you therefore, brothers, by the mercies of God, to present your bodies as a living sacrifice, holy and acceptable to God, which is your spiritual worship" (or "reasonable service"; KJV). It is reasonable that God calls us to service, and it is reasonable that we submit to God's calling us to service.

There are no exception clauses for Christian service. There's no "fine print" that excuses anyone from kingdom work. We never read, "But this does not apply to you if you are too young, too old, too busy, have too many other commitments, or if you have a mental illness." All members of Christ's body are called to service.

God's call to salvation
is also God's call to service.

So, what can a person with mental illness do?

Every Christian Has God-Given Gifts

Each member of Christ's church has been given spiritual gifts by God for his glory and for the edification of his church (Rom. 12:6–8). That includes those who suffer, although obviously their sufferings will limit to some degree the opportunities and possibilities of exercising these gifts.

Some have been given many gifts; some have been given few gifts. Some have been given more prominent or noticeable gifts; others' gifts may be less noticeable (but not less valuable). Some believers' gifts and functions in ministry are like hands or mouths (easy to see and appreciate); others are more like the toenail on our little toe. Although it is little noticed and rarely thought of, it helps protect the foot and whole body from harm, and the whole body is hampered when it is hurt or missing.

We are to use our gifts to care for the other members of Christ's church. The sufferer should therefore be asked, "In what ways can you use your gifts to serve others in the church or the community?" Another question for down the road is, "What gifts has your experience of mental illness developed in you?" God uses suffering to identify and develop gifts. Some of the most empathetic counselors are those who have suffered themselves (2 Cor. 1:3–7).

Suffering is better training
than studying.

But the person can hardly do anything for any length of time. What's the point in even trying?

Every Christian Blesses and Is Blessed in Serving

When a Christian is not serving, it's not only the church that misses out on blessing; so does the person. When God has given gifts but they are not being exercised, discouragement and a sense of worthlessness sets in. Conversely, when we take responsibility and invest in others, it shifts our focus away from our own pain toward alleviating the pain of others in a life of obedience and service.

While doing our duties and serving others does not take away mental illness, it can interrupt, distract from, and reduce irrational and painful thoughts that fuel mental illness. When all a sufferer has to focus on is the pain of the illness, the pain usually gets worse. When sufferers have other duties to motivate and orient their life, they experience some reprieve from the ravages and pain of their illness.

In the same way as weary parents experiencing the discomfort of muscle aches and tiredness muster up strength, get up out of bed, take care of their little ones and, in the process, experience energy and fulfillment, so responsibility can help motivate positive action and provide a sense of usefulness in the life of those suffering with mental illness. In many cases, sufferers are missing a sense of purpose and meaning in their everyday lives which leads to discouragement and isolation, further multiplying the effects of mental illness.

In addition to the psychological benefits of focusing on others, serving others, and finding purpose in the exercise of God-given gifts, there's also the spiritual benefit of God's blessing on top of all that. As the parable of the talents reveals, God adds his blessing when we obey him, do our duty, and exercise our gifts for his glory (Matt. 25:14–30).

While the ultimate goal is for every Christian to serve in God's kingdom and to be an active member of a local church, however, it may not always be best to start with the insistence that an individual with mental illness must serve in his local church congregation. Due to fears of rejection and embarrassment (and perhaps a previous history of rejection), it may be advisable to begin small and build slowly.

When we bless others,
God blesses us.

SUMMARY

Problem: Sufferers tend to miss out or pass on serving opportunities in the church.

Insights: Every Christian (1) serves God and his church, (2) has God-given gifts, and (3) blesses and is blessed in serving.

Action: Help the sufferer serve the church of Christ with their gifts.

- Read Romans 12:6–8; 1 Cor. 12:8–10, 28–30; and 1 Peter 4:11 with sufferers and ask them which gifts God has given them.
- Discern how sufferers have served God in the past and guide them as to how they might do so in modified form during this time of suffering.
- Talk about what gifts and graces God may be developing in this time of suffering.
- What might a graduated approach to serving look like? What would be step 1, step 2, step 3, etc.?
- Once a person has taken a step, help her to identify in what ways it made her feel better.
- Talk to church leaders about how sufferers might be given opportunities to serve.

Tom's Story

Several years ago, a pastor who was preaching in our congregation offered a perspective on God's grace and plan in our suffering: "God is fine-tuning your voice to sing the unique part in his choir, both on earth and in heaven, that glorifies Christ, a part you only can sing." Suffering can itself be service if it is offered to God in a humble, submissive spirit.

It's only through personal suffering, including depression, that I have been equipped to better serve others in my clinical practice and in my local church congregation. I have witnessed the initial surprise and then relief when those I am serving realize that my understanding and interventions with them are not coming from a textbook but rather from my own history of struggle and healing.

22

What Are the Biggest Challenges
in Discipling a Sufferer?

WE WANT TO SEE spiritual growth in sufferers, and we want to
see them serving in the church. But we have to face up to the fact
that discipling a sufferer runs into many challenges and problems.
Our too-high expectations can clash with their too-low expectations, leading to discouragement, distrust, and short-term ups and
downs. There are some big challenges, but they can be overcome.
Let's look at what will help discipleship.

Agreed Expectations Are Essential

Our expectations can be too high. Just as the first-time parent
learns to lower expectations for their parenting and their child, so
it is with mental illness. We need to take account of the condition
of the sufferer and adjust expectations accordingly.

While we may aim too high, the sufferer tends to aim too low.
They have a limited view of their potential and of God's power.
Given this clash of expectations, it's important for sufferers and
those involved in their care to talk about what is achievable and

come to some agreement about that from time to time as the person's condition changes. Ultimately, God must come into the picture here too, so that the sufferer does not despair and the caregivers are not too self-reliant.

One important area to discuss is frequency of care and meetings. We have to avoid being on call 24/7, but we also have to avoid sporadic and reactionary involvement. Agree on when meetings will take place and how long they will last, and do everything you can to make that a regular part of the sufferer's schedule. This will help them and will protect you as well. Caregivers need to know what their minds and bodies can handle and pace themselves accordingly.

Sufferers will have periods of thriving and stability, but they will also have periods of unpredictability and destabilization. They may need to go back to the inpatient psychiatric hospital. They may need to have their medications changed or the doses adjusted. This is not a failure on the caregiver or the sufferer's part, so don't let false guilt add additional pain to this situation.

Great expectations
will produce great disappointments.

How soon can I expect to see fruit?

Long-Haul Patience Is Essential

In dealing with people with a mental illness, it usually takes a long time to gain their trust and to get to know them personally, much longer than with someone who is well. Just as you cannot forcibly open a rose bud and expect good results, in the same way rushing a person struggling with thoughts and fears related to their mental illness will not produce good results. Often it will drive the person into isolation and emotional or physical withdrawal. The more patient we are in getting to know a person, the more likely he will be to trust and open up.

When we are impatient, we will not get to know the heart of those who suffer, and they will feel misunderstood and disrespected. We may try to mold them into something we would want them to be rather than who or what they are. They will then fear that they are not able or likely to live up to our expectations and will build emotional walls so that we are not able to get to know them or be allowed to be a part of their lives. Impatience produces distrust and withdrawal.

Part of forming realistic expectations is patience and a willingness to listen; when you think you are done listening, keep listening. This will help your understanding of those under your care: who they are as individual creations of God, how they relate emotionally, how they are dealing with their illness. People will not care how much you know until they know how much you care. So, take care and take caution: getting to know a person suffering with mental illness is not something that is accomplished in hours, days, or sometimes even in months. This is done over years and decades.

Discipling a healthy person takes a lot of time, and where there is mental illness it will usually take even longer. There will be starts and stops, twists and turns, unexpected roadblocks and detours, and extra layers of complexity. But there will also be more growth that goes unseen, growth that evidences itself rather unexpectedly. You may find yourself wondering, "Will they ever get it?" and the next day, "Wow, I didn't think so, but they are catching on way more than I ever thought."

---

*Patience helps
and heals the patient.*

What should be my short-term expectations?

A Flexible Outlook Is Essential

A flexible outlook is something we all eventually adopt when we are dealing with someone experiencing a major physical illness, such as cancer. There may be days when the person with cancer is feeling well and may appear extremely healthy. Then, mere hours later, without much warning, they may be writhing in pain. We adjust our expectations and how we deal with them based on how the illness is affecting them. We need this kind of sensitive daily adjustment of expectations, as determined by the condition of the sufferer.

In dealing with a person with cancer, during periods of recovery and stability, a longer visit with more in-depth conversation may well take place. However, when the pain of the cancer returns, the visit may be cut short and the conversation may be kept on the surface. We offer only brief words of comfort or encouragement. This is also the case in mental illness: where someone is in the cycle and severity of the illness will determine what they are prepared for and are needing. Remaining patient, open, and flexible to what sufferers are capable of and needing will enhance your ability to emotionally connect with and minister to them.

Flexibility
is a valuable ability.

SUMMARY

Problem: Discipling a sufferer runs into many challenges and problems.

Insights: (1) Agreed expectations, (2) long-haul patience, and (3) short-term flexibility are all essential.

Action: Disciple sufferers despite the challenges of expectations, impatience, and changes.

- Initiate discussion of expectations regarding number and length of meetings.
- Schedule regular times so that the person knows you will be available to talk at that time.
- Think about what graces God is growing in you during the time (sympathy? patience? love?).
- Consider what you will look for to decide how much a person is up to each day.

David's Story

By the time mental illness is diagnosed or recognized and accepted, the person's spiritual life is usually already suffering. Both Shona and I found that, in the first couple of weeks after accepting the reality of our own depressions, a short daily check-in was helpful. We usually did this at the same time every day (just after supper, with a cup of tea). We would list positives in the day, note one or two negatives, read a few Bible verses, talk about them, and pray together. Usually this was no more than 10 or 15 minutes, but if our time together included an especially important conversation, then we would be flexible with our time to get the most benefit from the discussion. As the weeks passed, this time became shorter and then we agreed to move to three times a week, then weekly, as our conditions improved.

We found this was a good way to avoid ignoring the problem, but by limiting the time and frequency of discussions, we managed to avoid its becoming everything in our lives and relationship. We also had a general structure for meetings that enabled us to stay on track and measure progress for our own encouragement. When we had an especially discouraging review of the day, we would then be able to remind ourselves of previous daily reviews that indicated long-term progress.

23

What Are the Roles of Scripture, Prayer, and the Sacraments in a Sufferer's Life?

EVERYONE HAS DOWNS in their spiritual life, but, with mental illness, the downs are deeper and longer. Scripture is harder to read, believe, and act upon. Sufferers give up on prayer, stay away from the Lord's Table, and withdraw from fellowship. God, though, has provided these means of grace to bring grace into the lives of all of us, especially sufferers. So, let's look at the role of the means of grace in a sufferer's life.

The Means of Grace Remain the Means of Grace

No matter what our mental or emotional state, we need grace, and, therefore, we need the means of grace that God has appointed. We cannot begin to heal or rebuild without them.

When it comes to Scripture, as Jesus said, we cannot live by bread alone but by every word that proceeds out of the mouth of God (Matt. 4:4; Deut. 8:3). The mentally ill need God's word as much as, if not more than, daily food, if they want to live spiritually. It not only speaks to immediate needs and challenges but also builds long-term strength and an accurate worldview.

Prayer is not only an expression of need and dependence on God, it's also the way we receive help and support from God. As mental illness creates such weakness and need, prayer is vital to providing for these needs. Prayer brings us into God's presence and unites us with God, connecting us with his power and mercy, as well as reorienting us to view ourselves and the world differently. In church, we have the benefit of someone praying the words and our simply following along, which is much easier for sufferers than having to form our own prayers in private.

The Lord's Supper also brings us into communion with the Lord and brings his presence to us through the bread and wine. These elements remind us of the objective truths of the cross and resurrection, God's desire to feast and fellowship with us, and the unity we have with other Christians in God's family. Baptism is also a help, even when it is being administered to others. Again, it gives objective form to the truths of God, which is always helpful to those with mental illness, whose sense of objectivity is malfunctioning. If we are paedobaptists, baptism reminds us of God's covenant promises to us and our children. If we are credobaptists, it reminds us of God's work in our lives and our previous testimony to it.

One of the most common themes we've heard from Christians who have suffered with mental illness is the importance of singing praise to God, not only privately but also publicly. There's something wonderfully therapeutic about praising God in public worship; not just reading, and not just hearing the word of God, but singing it and its truths. Music, especially the human voice, gets truth deeper and makes it last longer. The Psalms are especially helpful here as they balance divine revelation and the honest expression of human emotion in all its height, depth, and breadth. While giving us words with which to articulate our feelings, songs also lead us toward the transformation of our emotions. Songs lift us into the presence of the heavenly church as we join their choir of praise to our God.

Mental illness is often a lonely experience, isolating and distancing us from others. We want to withdraw from people, and sometimes people want to withdraw from us. However, the church is a family that welcomes the broken and the bruised, providing friendship and fellowship. We need to be among God's people because we need them, and even more importantly, they need us and miss us when we are not there.

We will miss out on grace
if we miss out on the means of grace.

"This is all very well and true," you say, "but do you not understand the extra difficulties sufferers face when it comes to the means of grace?"

We agree, there are difficulties, additional obstacles, in the way of the mentally ill. Let's look at a few of them before proposing some solutions.

The Means of Grace Face Additional Obstacles

Although God has appointed the means of grace to bring his grace to us, this does not automatically happen. Even those who are mentally and emotionally thriving can have difficulties in accessing and receiving the grace God makes available to them. These difficulties and obstacles are even greater for the mentally ill.

Depending on the severity of the mental illness, sufferers will to one degree or another be impaired in their ability to think. They will find it hard to concentrate, easy to be distracted, difficult to follow arguments, and tough to remember what was read or heard. They will be cognitively lethargic, or, if mania is present, then the opposite will be the case. They will find it too hard to slow their thoughts down to think on what they are hearing. With schizophrenia, there may be voices within that prevent them from thinking about any external voice in their lives.

Even when they do manage to connect with what they are reading or hearing, they can feel cold and lifeless in their response. Truths that used to thrill and excite them leave them untouched and apathetic. Even worship songs that used to warm them, leave them cold. The lack of feeling also affects their thinking, because if they are not excited and emotionally invested, concentration is also affected.

When thinking and feeling is affected, so, obviously, will their faith be affected. Faith uses these other faculties and, therefore, will be damaged when those faculties are damaged. But there's also the problem that cynicism and suspicion can increase in mental illness. That makes it hard to believe and trust other people and to trust God, especially his goodness and love. Those who suffer may believe in God's mercy in general, but it's for everyone else, not for them. They may avoid the Lord's Table, believing it's not for them.

All that being true, it is inevitable that the sufferer's ability to act on what they read or hear or sing is also impaired. Even when they can think and feel and believe, they are physically tired and volitionally weak. They want to do, but feel low on "doing power."

The sufferer may have tried and failed many times before and, therefore, simply feels it doesn't help.

Lack of faith is rarely the
cause of mental illness
but it's often the effect of mental illness.

So what should sufferers do? If they need the means of grace, and yet face additional obstacles, how can I help them?

The Means of Grace Need Additional Support

Although it may sound strange, the answer to such spiritual problems will often begin with physical solutions. Getting healthier overall will help sufferers spiritually. Working on other areas of their lives such as diet, exercise, sleep, daily routines, or hobbies, together with medications, can improve overall health and faculties, which will also benefit their spiritual lives.

No one can beat this alone. If sufferers simply focus only on things like private Bible-reading, prayer, or singing, or watching sermons online, they deprive themselves of the human support they so much need. By asking a family member or friend to read, pray, or sing with them, they will see how the presence of even one other person can bring additional life to spiritual disciplines.

Mental illness is not a time to be reading unfamiliar Bible books. Better to stick to the simpler and more familiar passages where the sufferer has met God before. It will take less mental effort and hopefully remind them of past mercies. But we don't want them only to look backward; we want them to look forward too. Talk about what you look forward to, or what you would like the future to look like, and ask them to do the same. And think together about your eternal future and what that experience will be like.

All of these additional supports can overcome the additional obstacles and provide additional blessing along with the means of grace. God's strength is made perfect in our weakness, and he is glorified in and through it all.

---

*Mental illness is hard for us,
but nothing is too hard for God.*

SUMMARY

Problem: Everyone has downs in their spiritual life, but with mental illness the downs are deeper and longer.

Insights: For those with mental illness, the means of grace (1) remain the means of grace, (2) face additional obstacles, and (3) need additional supports.

Action: Help the sufferer use the ordinary means of grace in public and private.

- Talk with sufferers about the extra difficulties they face in relation to the means of grace. Express sympathy for their situation.

- Discuss how important the ordinary means of grace are, and help the sufferer make plans for establishing and continuing routines and patterns of Bible reading, prayer, church attendance, fellowship, and praise.
- If the sufferer is not going out to church, bring church to him or her as much as you can.
- Help the sufferer look backward to God's goodness and look forward with hope in God's promises.
- Raymond Edman (former president of Wheaton College), in expounding Isaiah 50:10 instructed, "Never doubt in the dark what God has told you in the light."[1] How does this apply to mental illness?

David's Story

There were times in my life when I did not want to take part in fellowship with people after church. I would find a way to get out of the building as quickly as possible and park in a place that no one would see me and come to talk to me, no matter how long Shona was talking to people. I just wanted to get away from people and go home. Shona often challenged me on this, but I continued in my self-isolation. I was social distancing before the days of social distancing! I wasn't a pastor at that time, simply a church member, which made it easier for me to withdraw without anyone questioning where I was.

1   V. Raymond Edman, *The Disciplines of Life* (Wheaton, IL: Van Kampen, 1948).

One of the biggest changes for me when antidepressants started working in my life, was a desire to be with God's people again. It wasn't immediate, but over time I found myself looking forward to church again. It also coincided with moving to a new church which used more modern worship songs and hymns (I had been worshiping in churches that used only old Psalm versions). Nothing healed me more than public worship, especially singing Christ-full songs with God's people. To this day, corporate singing is a vital part of maintaining my mental health.

24

What Are Some Things to Avoid in Ministering to Sufferers?

WE MAKE MANY MISTAKES in what we say to sufferers. Partly because of ignorance, discomfort, or fear, we end up saying nothing, or nothing helpful, or everything wrong. These are all pitfalls to avoid, so let's look at them more closely and explore how to make our words healing bridges rather than damaging holes.

Common Pitfalls Are Silence, Platitudes, and Error

Some of the biggest pitfalls to avoid are silence, platitudes, and mistakes.

Silence is a pitfall. Although there are times when silence is appropriate, too much of it is unhelpful to the mentally ill. That's because they will often misinterpret silence as lack of love, concern, or sympathy. They may even read criticism into your silence. Another way of silence harming the mentally ill is when we simply avoid them. We don't visit them, or we don't stop and talk with them. Again, this silence does not go unnoticed and can add to the suffering.

Platitudes are a pitfall. The second worst thing to silence is clichés and platitudes. Pep talks and patronizing advice are agonies. These usually come in one of three categories. The first category is false promises, which means assuring people of quick and easy recovery with no basis in fact. "You will be better soon . . . This will pass . . . You'll get over it . . . This will be sanctified to you . . . I know how you feel . . ."

The second category of platitudes is false equivalents, which is when we compare sufferers to others, usually unfavorably. "There are others worse off . . . It could be worse . . . I know somebody else with this . . ." When a person is mentally ill, it often feels like there's no one else in the world like this. Comparing them to others only makes them feel worse.

The third category of platitudes is false "shoulds," which impose obligations on people or set unrealistic expectations. "You should get out more . . . You should stop taking meds . . . You should repent . . . You should trust God more . . ." Many mentally ill people already impose a huge number of false "shoulds" on themselves, and therefore this only increases the pain. "Should" or "ought to" statements convey a sense of superiority of the speaker to the inferior sufferer, resulting in more shame and alienation.

All of these are platitudes that people hear in other contexts and just thoughtlessly apply to this unique situation without considering how devastating they can be.

Error is a pitfall. The greatest error we can make is condemnation. Usually, the worst thing you can do is criticize people with mental illness, tell them that they are to blame, they are guilty, they are weak, they are not being Christian, and so on. In many cases it's like blaming someone for having cancer or diabetes. It is grossly unfair and heaps false guilt on top of everything else.

The second error is that of amateur diagnosis. One thing the mentally ill often have to contend with is people who know nothing volunteering or even forcing their own diagnoses and prescriptions on them. They pick up pieces of information in popular culture or on websites, or from some extremist or other, and then use that little knowledge to attempt to cure someone with mental illness. This is not only foolish; it's dangerous.

Unhelpful words
are no help to the helpless.

We don't want to fall into any of these pitfalls, do we? So, if these are the negatives, what are the positives? If these are pitfalls to avoid, what are the ways to build bridges?

Good Bridges Are Confession, Learning, and Prayer

First, *admit the difficulty*. Confess to God and to sufferers that we've made mistakes in the past, we've fallen into pitfalls, but we want to be constructive, not destructive, going forward. Talk to the person and "say sorry" for wrongs done and said in the past. Ask them for help to speak wisely and helpfully into their lives. "I don't know what to say, and I wish I had some really good advice. Just know that I care and will be praying for you." Give them permission to let you know when you are being helpful or unhelpful. Pray for wisdom from above to speak wisely and winningly so that no one loses.

Second, *learn from others.* Talk to friends and family of other mentally ill people and ask them what they've found works and what doesn't. Get permission to talk to any counselor in your loved one's life and ask them how you can support their work. What you will hear will guide you. For example, you may be advised to

- Listen before you speak.
- Ask questions before you give answers.
- Support and reinforce counseling.
- Gently offer hope and encouragement.
- Learn from mistakes.
- Speak quietly and slowly.
- Share from your study.
- Turn to positives.
- Admire and encourage what is good.

Third, *ask God to help you speak,* to help you speak truth, and to help you speak lovingly. Ask him for love to make you seek out the mentally ill and spend time with them. Pray that your words will be healing rather than wounding. Remember this great promise: "If any of you lacks wisdom, let him ask God, who gives generously to all without reproach, and it will be given him" (James 1:5).

---

*Build bridges
to build relationships.*

SUMMARY

Problem: Because of ignorance, discomfort, and fear, we make mistakes in what we say to sufferers.

Insights: (1) Common pitfalls are silence, platitudes, and errors. (2) Good bridges are confession, learning, and prayer.

Action: Admit the difficulty (to God, self, and sufferers), avoid the speech pitfalls, and build speech bridges.

- Ask your loved one what words wound and what words heal.
- Ask a counselor or doctor or pastor what words are helpful to sufferers.
- When you are about to speak, ask, "Will this build a bridge or dig a pit?"

David's Story

When Shona suffered the deep depression around the birth of our fourth child, as described in the story at the end of chapter 19, I remember trying to reason with her night after night while sitting on the sofa. I hadn't yet understood the nature of depression nor how to respond to it and thought that facts could change her feelings. Eventually, after I had made my best arguments for why she should not be depressed, and had piled up multiple reasons why she should be happy, she turned to me with tears streaming down her face and pleaded, "David, would you just put your arm around me?" She didn't need words and logic at that point; she needed love, warmth, connection, and acceptance. From then on, I prioritized love before logic, silence before speaking, and strong affection before strong arguments. That was a big turning point for both of us in overcoming her depression.

25

What Should We Do When a Sufferer Falls into Temptation?

THOSE WHO SUFFER with mental illness are no different than anyone else in that they are sinners who fall into sin. However, they will often fall into greater sin and fall into sin repeatedly due to their mental and emotional weakness. The question is, how do we react to this?

It's easy to react with pride: "I'd never do that." Like the Pharisee, we are tempted to think ourselves better or stronger than others. Or we may go further and respond with condemnation: "If you were a Christian, you'd never be like that." But we can also go to the other extreme and overlook sin: "It doesn't matter, you're not well." Or we can just give up on a person: "I suppose this is the new normal."

None of these reactions help the sufferer, so what should we remember when someone with mental illness sins?

Remember Your Own Weakness

We begin by reminding ourselves that, unlike our suffering friend or family member, we are well, we are healthy, and we have all our faculties and abilities. We are not laboring against the same mental and emotional disabilities and difficulties. And yet, despite our general overall health, we are still sinners and we still sin. If we don't fall into really serious sin, it is only by God's grace. Remembering how weak we are, morally and spiritually, even when in perfect health, is the safest platform from which to address sin in others. As the apostle Paul said, "Brothers, if anyone is caught in any transgression, you who are spiritual should restore him in a spirit of gentleness. Keep watch on yourself, lest you too be tempted" (Gal. 6:1).

Self-confidence is dangerous not only to those we are trying to help but to ourselves as well. For example, in Daniel 4, King Nebuchadnezzar foolishly and proudly attributed all his success to his own doing, but in a moment, his reasoning and strength were taken from him; he spent a considerable amount of time being humbled and learning the lesson that anything he had or accomplished were gifts from God. When urging the Corinthian church to correct sinners, Paul reminded them, "let anyone who thinks that he stands take heed lest he fall" (1 Cor. 10:12).

As we approach a sufferer who has fallen into sin, we want to ask ourselves these questions before we ask the sufferer any questions: "For who sees anything different in you? What do you have that you did not receive? If then you received it, why do you boast as if you did not receive it?" (1 Cor. 4:7).

---

*Remembering our weakness
is the best way to spiritual strength.*

"But even in my weakest moment, I wouldn't do that," you may argue.

Remember the Sufferer's Weakness

While that thought may result from not realizing how weak you are, it may also result from your not realizing how weak the sufferer is. When we've not experienced mental illness, it can be difficult for us to understand how confused and irrational the mind can be, and how unpredictable and uncontrollable the feelings may be. This can lead to unrealistic expectations in us, especially as a person begins to recover from mental illness.

Many times, these expectations come in the form of what we tell ourselves "should be," "could be," or "would be." Sometimes these are referred to as "shoulda, coulda, woulda," the terrible triplets that always bring disappointment and devastation. Recognizing these terrible triplets for the liars that they are can help protect our minds and emotions from their damaging impact.

If we think of recovery as a simple and uncomplicated process, we will be disappointed. If we expect someone with a mental illness to learn a lesson quickly, we'll be disappointed. If we expect a person to learn a lesson and not have to relearn it or be reminded of it, we'll be disappointed. If we expect the journey to stability to be a linear process (no ups and downs, no detours, no setbacks or backsliding), we'll be disappointed.

Discipling any person requires patience and perseverance, as sometimes they take two steps backward for every one step forward. Sometimes they stall and stagnate for a while. They fall and fail, sometimes immediately after success and progress. If that's the case with healthy disciples, it's so much more the case with those who have a mental illness.

There will be stops and starts, gains and losses, hopes and disappointment. There will be days when all of our efforts will be unappreciated or resisted. There will be some days (or weeks or months) when the illness may cloud the person's perception to such a degree that those who love them and are trying to help them are perceived as enemies rather than allies. It will seem that all our effort has been wasted and has come to nothing.

Progress is never straight;
it's always a squiggle.

So far, we've considered our weakness and their weakness. Where can we get strength for us and them?

Remember God's Strength

Remember God's strong grace. How many times have we sinned and yet God has kept coming back to give us another chance? He has not given up on us or the sufferer, and therefore we should not give up either. Remember how many people in the New Testament Jesus took on who were hopeless cases.

Remember God's strong forgiveness. No matter how grievous the sin, how long the sin, how repeated the sin, how damaging the sin, God can still forgive fully, freely, and forever. If God can forgive the mentally ill, then so should we.

Remember God's strong restoration. God does not offer half-restoration but full restoration, full reconciliation, full rejoicing, full favor, and full fellowship.

Remember God's strong power. No matter how deep or strong a pattern of sin, God can deliver from it, God can break the pattern or habit. The weakest sinner caught in the strongest sin is no match for the almighty God. Look through biblical history, through church history, through your own history and see how strong God has been in so many weak people.

We are not depending on the sufferer's power, nor on our own power, but on God's power alone. He works through our work, but ultimately any success is by his Spirit, not ours.

Work hard
to trust hard in God's work.

Is there anyone who modeled this kind of patient and powerful caregiving that we can follow?

Remember Jesus's Salvation

No one knows how long, hard, and arduous the process of discipling is like our Lord Jesus. At the beginning of his public ministry, he called twelve men from various walks of life to follow him. He spent three whole years walking, talking, teaching, eating, and serving with them. They watched him perform miracles of physical and spiritual healing. They heard every one of his sermons and personal conversations. Yet when it came to his very last night on earth, he found them arguing as to which of them Jesus liked best and which of them was most important.

We might expect a sigh of disappointment, or an exasperated rebuke. But, ever patient and kind, Jesus took a basin and towel and began washing his disciples' feet and encouraging them to do the same for others. He addressed their sin, called them to repentance, showed how ready he was to welcome and wash sinners, and pointed them again to the way of holiness (John 13:1–17). What a model!

In discipling a person with mental illness, we will experience disappointment, frustration, and weariness. We may wonder, "Will they ever get it? Has this person not listened to or learned anything from what I have been saying and working on all this time?" Remembering Jesus will remind us to address sin and not overlook it; to call to repentance and not make excuses for sin; to point people to forgiveness and cleansing rather than driving them to guilty despair; and to encourage in the way of holiness rather than giving up on it.

No one moves from selfish sin
to selfless serving
without going to Jesus for
his selfless salvation.

SUMMARY

Problem: We react wrongly when people with mental illness fall into sin.

Insights: Remember (1) your own weakness, (2) the sufferer's weakness, (3) God's strength, and (4) Jesus's salvation.

Action: Remember your weakness, the sufferer's weakness, God's strength, and Christ's salvation when sufferers sin.

- Be on the lookout for Pharisaical pride, condemning without grace, ignoring sin, and defeatism.
- Take some time to remember your own weakest moments, even when you were healthy.
- Draw a graphic of your own discipleship with its ups and downs, twists and turns, falls and fails.
- Point sufferers to God's strength and Jesus's salvation.
- Think about how you can live out John 13:1–17 in the lives of sufferers.

David's Story

Whether sin has caused a particular person's depression, it is always the result of any depression. Even when I came to accept that not all depression was the result of sin, I was still lacking in sympathy for those who fell into sin while in depression. I couldn't understand how easily, quickly, and repeatedly the mentally ill could sin.

That was until I experienced depression and anxiety myself. I hardly slept for weeks and as a result was extremely weak spiritually. But Shona still held me to account. She was kind but firm in encouraging me to take responsibility in the family, and not to use my condition as an excuse to check out of my duties.

Now, having been through it myself, I am much gentler with the mentally ill, but I still don't mollycoddle them. I don't impatiently or angrily condemn them, but I quietly and kindly point out sin and point them to the cross for forgiveness of sin, and to the Holy Spirit for power over sin.

26

How Can We Help Someone
Who Is Suicidal?

SUICIDE IS A LEADING cause of death in the USA, resulting in more than 48,000 deaths in 2018. That's the highest suicide rate in 30 years. Suicide was the second leading cause of death among individuals between the ages of 10 and 34, and the fourth leading cause of death among individuals between the ages of 35 and 54. In 2018, there were more than two and a half times as many suicides (48,344) in the United States as there were homicides (18,830).[1] Depression is the key indicator in two thirds of all suicides, with other key indicators being childhood abuse and confusion over sexuality. Psychotic illnesses also carry a higher risk of suicide. Eating disorders such as anorexia are also associated with increased suicide risk due to the impact of starvation on the mind and mood. If we want to be good at caring, we need to face up to the painful reality of suicidal thoughts in those we care for and be equipped to help them in that darkness.

1   "Suicide," *National Institute of Mental Health*, accessed March 31, 2022, https://www.nimh.nih.gov/health/statistics/suicide.shtml.

Know the Signs

So how do I know if someone is thinking about suicide? The National Suicide Prevention Lifeline says three major signs of immediate suicide risk are: (1) talking about wanting to die or to kill oneself; (2) looking for a way to kill oneself, such as searching online or obtaining a gun; (3) talking about feeling hopeless or having no reason to live. Other behaviors may also indicate a serious risk, especially if the behavior is new, has increased, or seems related to a painful event, loss, or change (e.g., withdrawing or isolating oneself, extreme mood swings, sleeping too much or too little, acting recklessly, abuse of alcohol or drugs, and expressions of despair).[2]

There are several levels of risk, and although you are probably not best placed to determine for sure where to put someone on that list, here are the broad outlines:

- *Level 1.* The general wish to be dead, without any thoughts of harming yourself (this should still be taken seriously, but is a lower risk than the other levels).
- *Level 2.* The presence of thoughts to kill yourself without any thoughts of *how* you might kill yourself.
- *Level 3.* The presence of a method. This is a general idea only, without specific details or any wish to actually carry it out (i.e., the thoughts may feel quite alien to the person).
- *Level 4.* The presence of some intent to actually kill yourself, but without specific plans.

2 "We Can All Prevent Suicide," *Suicide Prevention Lifeline*, accessed March 31, 2022, https://suicidepreventionlifeline.org/how-we-can-all-prevent-suicide/.

• *Level 5.* The presence of a detailed plan with methods, timing, and some form of plan to carry it out.

---

*Know the signs
to notice the signs.*

If I see worrying signs, what should I say?

Know What to Say

Although it's counterintuitive, the most important thing to do is to ask the person if he is thinking about taking his life. Do so in a nonthreatening, nonconfrontational way, to make it as easy as possible for him to speak openly about his thoughts and feelings. Perhaps you can begin with some general questions such as,

- How have you been feeling in your mood recently?
- What's been on your mind lately?
- Are you sleeping okay?
- Are you eating okay?
- How are your stress levels?
- Are you able to get things done, or is it all getting a bit much?
- Are you hopeful about the future?

Hopefully this will establish trust and confidence and allow you to press closer and deeper with a question phrased something like this: "I see you're hurting very deeply. I'm so sorry and really want to help. Is it bad enough that you've been thinking about taking your own life?" Rather than planting suicidal thoughts in his mind, this may allow the suicidal person to admit it and to seek professional help. This is vital and urgent if he tells you that he has got to the stage of making a plan.

As you pursue professional help, you can present reasons why the person should not take another step in that direction. For example, in *Broken Minds*, Pastor Steve Bloem gives a number of reasons he has, at times, used to convince himself not to commit suicide:

- It is a sin and would bring shame to Christ and his church.
- It would please the devil and would weaken greatly those who are trying to fight him.
- It would devastate family members and friends, and you may be responsible for their following your example if they come up against intense suffering.
- It may not work, and you could end up severely disabled but still trying to fight depression.
- It is true—our God is a refuge (Ps. 46:1).
- Help is available. If you push hard enough, someone can assist you to find the help you need.
- If you are unsaved, you will go to hell. This is not because of the act of suicide but because all who die apart from knowing Christ personally will face an eternity in a far worse situation than depression.
- If you are a Christian, then Jesus Christ is interceding for you, that your faith will not fail.
- God will keep you until you reach a day when your pain will truly be over.[3]

3 Steve and Robyn Bloem, *Broken Minds: Hope for Healing When You Feel Like You're Losing It* (Grand Rapids, MI: Kregel, 2005), 59–60.

When using these reasons with someone else, you could turn them into questions so that they are more expressions of concern than condemnation.

Hard questions
can be healing questions.

If I'm alarmed by the answers or nonanswers to my questions, what should I do?

Know What to Do

If you're afraid that someone may be considering suicide, it's imperative to reach out for help and not try to manage it alone. There are three choices here, depending on the seriousness of the situation and the refusal of the person to cooperate:

- Call a suicide crisis line: 1-800-273-TALK (8255).
- Take the person to the emergency room.
- Call 911.

When a suicidal person returns home, follow up with counseling appointments and ensure that they attend. Ask them to agree to safety and sobriety measures, and remove guns, knives, drugs, pills, ropes from the environment. Keep supporting them and surrounding them with friends and family. A sense of connectedness is an important component in cultivating a desire to live. Work with the person to develop a safety plan with concrete steps to take if suicidal thoughts return.

Overreaction
is safer than underreaction.

SUMMARY

Problem: Although suicide rates are increasing and mental illness is a key indicator for it, we lack the desire and the ability to talk with or help someone with suicidal thoughts.

Insights: (1) Know the signs. (2) Know what to say. (3) Know what to do.

Action: Be proactive in initiating conversation about suicide and be prepared to do what's necessary to keep the person safe.

- Visit websites like *The Suicide Prevention Lifeline* and *Be the One to Help Save a Life.*[4]
- Call a suicide helpline and ask them to guide you through their recommended best practices.
- Know where the nearest ER is, and find out if it includes a psychiatric ER.
- Learn how to initiate a nonthreatening conversation about suicide.
- Prepare a safety plan with someone you feel is at risk.

---

4 National Suicide Prevention Hotline, https://suicidepreventionlifeline.org/; and, "Be the One to Help Save a Life," *BeThe1To*, https://www.bethe1to.com/.

Tom's Story about Heather

Greta had that uneasy feeling. She was worried. Her friend Heather seemed so distant, so detached, and so down. She feared that suicide may be on Heather's mind. Greta didn't want to make it worse, but she knew that to not say anything would be the decision she would live to regret. After agonizing over how to bring up this very personal and sensitive emotional issue, Greta finally made the decision to ask Heather about depression and suicidal thoughts. Greta noticed a huge lump in her throat and heart beating out of her chest as she approached Heather.

It did not go as planned. It certainly was not an all-star performance, but Greta cared enough to ask about Heather's struggle and gave her the opportunity for discussing the severity of her condition. Several months later, Heather confessed that Greta's compassion and courage to address this "saved my life."

27

How Can We Care for Caregivers?

THE VERY FACT of your reading this book would suggest that either you are presently in a helping or caring role, or you are trying to figure out what your role should be. You therefore have felt to some degree the weight of this role. Realizing it is a physically, emotionally, and spiritually demanding calling, you are looking for help to support those that struggle with mental illness. But whether you are a parent, a spouse, a child, a friend, or a pastor, you also need help for yourself.

Too many times we've seen family, friends, elders, and pastors neglect themselves and their own needs, thinking that's the way to better serve others. But they've failed to realize that they are not machines that can operate tirelessly without any break, without any emotional, physical, or spiritual refueling. The end result is they become weary and ultimately ineffective. They may still be going through the motions, but they are expending more and more effort to realize less and less positive outcomes. This is especially because, in these situations, caregiving often lasts a long time and gradually involves more and more responsibility and time. Exhaustion leads to burnout and maybe even mental illness for the caregiver too.

No matter how capable the helper, everyone has limits. Eventually, the caregivers need to be cared for. They need others to come alongside them. Let's look at what we can do to care for the caregivers.

Caregivers Need Prayer

We can pray for caregivers. Even when the mentally ill are prayed for in church and by others, we often forget to pray for those caring for them with all the stress and demands that involves. As Aaron and Hur held up Moses's hands on top of the hill while the Israelites fought the Amalekites, so caregivers also need others propping them up in prayer.

We can also pray *with* the caregiver: It's one thing to pray for them, and even to tell them that you are praying for them, but it's best of all to take time out to pray with them, to get alongside them in their home, or at church, and to ask what to pray for and then to pray along those lines.

The best praying is caring,
and the best caring is praying.

Can we do more than pray?

Caregivers Need Support

Obviously, it's easy to pray and walk away. But caregivers need more than that. They need practical support. Support by offering a listening ear, because they will rarely have that in the sufferer.

Support by asking what their challenges and needs are and then trying to meet those needs. Support by telling them that their service is God's service, that it is their calling, and that they are pleasing God in it. Support by offering them a time of fellowship away from the sufferer, or by offering to watch the sufferer while they go out with a spouse or friends. Support by buying them groceries from time to time or even by bringing them meals. Support by enabling them to go to church, prayer meetings, Bible studies. Support by sending them devotional thoughts and sharing Bible readings together. In these and other ways, we can help caregivers feel supported by knowing they are not alone in this. Thankfully, Lifeway's research found that 75 percent of family members say the church has supported them, as have 53 percent of sufferers.[1]

Where caregivers are lacking,
we can provide backing.

How else can we help caregivers avoid burnout?

Caregivers Need Boundaries

In Exodus 18, Jethro saw that Moses was burning out because he had no boundaries to his desire to care for the Israelites. Jethro came alongside Moses and enabled him to see his limitations and where he could bring in others to help him. Caregivers may need their

---

1 *Serving Those with Mental Illness* (Colorado Springs: Focus on the Family, 2014), 8, https://media.focusonthefamily.com/pastoral/pdf/PAS_eBook_Series_Mental_Health _INTERACTIVE.pdf.

own "Jethros" in their life, an ally or partner to help them monitor their own physical, emotional, or spiritual needs, recognize their limits, and set boundaries.

As someone who also had a limited and weak humanity, even Jesus had to recognize his limits and set boundaries in his caregiving. He knew how to pace himself and how to take breaks. While the Gospels do give examples of the long hours Jesus put in (healing, teaching, interacting on a personal level), they also give examples of Jesus sending the crowds away (Matt. 14:22; 15:39; Luke 9). He got weary (emotionally), tired (physically), and drained (spiritually). He understood his limits and the need to set boundaries. There were times when he and his disciples retreated to the other side of the Jordan River to spend quiet time by themselves. They took boat rides across Lake Galilee. Jesus went to a mountain, by himself, to spend time with his heavenly Father. Jesus knew when it was time to take time out, to spend time with his friends, to spend time with his Father. We should not try to be more "Christian" than Jesus!

Jethro and Jesus give us permission to recognize limits and set boundaries. As it's hard to do this for ourselves, it is sometimes helpful for caregivers to give that boundary-setting role to someone else who can look at the situation more objectively and accurately.

*Recognizing limits and setting boundaries
is Christlike and Christian.*

SUMMARY

Problem: Caregivers need care if they are not to burn out.

Insights: Caregivers need (1) prayer, (2) support, and (3) boundaries.

Action: Care for the caregivers by prayer, support, and setting boundaries.

- Think about ways you can pray for and support caregivers.
- Discuss with caregivers what they think may be indicators of compassion fatigue or caregiver burnout.
- How would you help caregivers set physical, emotional, spiritual, and relational boundaries?

David's Story

We usually think of burnout only in terms of physical exhaustion, but there are two other dangers we need to watch for. The second danger is cynicism, often called "depersonalization." I've seen this happen a number of times and have experienced a degree of it myself in some situations. It's when we become detached from the people we work with or are caring for. Perhaps we are doubtful of their diagnoses, or cynical about how helpless they really are, or suspicious that they're not really trying to get better. We become negative and numb toward the person. This is not a physical drain so much as a psychological drain. Education about mental illness, what it is and what it's like to suffer with it, can help to reduce or remove cynicism and reenergize the caregiver.

The third danger is a sense of ineffectiveness. Caregivers feel ill-equipped to help, doubt they have the capabilities to perform this role, or don't feel confident about their competence. This is where training and encouragement can play big roles. We can provide resources and reassurance that they are doing a great job. We can help them see that they are not just spinning their wheels but are making progress.

So, when talking with caregivers, it's good to surface these three areas so as to help them avoid or recover from burnout.

28

How Can We Reduce the Stigma of Mental Illness?

MANY STILL VIEW the diagnosis of mental illness as a stigma. It's a mark of disgrace and shame, something to be embarrassed about, hide, and keep private. This is partly because of ignorance about its causes, partly because of negative and extreme caricatures presented by the entertainment industry, and partly because the church has often condemned mental illness as a sin or as always being caused by sin. Little wonder that people feel ashamed of it, scared of it, and guilty about it.

Thankfully, with more education in our schools, more sensitive portrayals in the media, and increased understanding in the church, the stigma is being reduced, albeit slowly. People are therefore more prepared to admit mental illness, talk about it, and seek help. But more can be done, and we want to look at what we can do.

Education Reduces Stigma

Education is key to understanding mental illness and banishing erroneous ideas. We therefore want to encourage people to read books, attend seminars, take courses, watch videos, and listen to mental health experts on this topic.

Give special attention to the latest medical research, which is finding much more of a physical and organic cause in mental illness. You will also find out about medications, what they can do and what they can't do.

A balanced study of the Psalms will help us see that depression and anxiety are normal abnormalities in an abnormal world. The Psalms will also encourage us that God moves his people through these dark and fearful times into the light and life of his love.

Increased information
reduces incrimination.

So, do I just read books and watch videos?

Investment in Lives Reduces Stigma

Perhaps the best way to remove stigma in our thinking, speaking, and acting, is to talk with the mentally ill. Tell them you don't understand their suffering very well, but that you want to understand it better. Try to listen with an open mind, without prejudging, condemning, or critiquing. You might find you have more in common than you think.

Ask them what is especially hurtful and how they have experienced the stigma of mental illness. They will probably describe things like cruel comments, proud smirks, exclusion from friend groups, lost job opportunities, rejected marriage proposals, discrimination, distrust, and so on. They've sometimes experienced so much stigmatization that even when it is not present around them, they still feel it inside. They stigmatize themselves, making them feel like damaged goods, like outsiders.

But also remember to talk about other aspects of their lives, so that you can see how much they are also trying to live a normal life. Mental illness does not usually define the totality of a person, and talking with them will help you see that they function well in many areas of life despite this disability.

Increased investment
reduces indictment.

Positive Results Reduce Stigma

In the last chapter of this book, we will expand upon the idea of the benefits of mental illness, but we want to mention it here as well, as this plays a role in reducing stigma. When we see how much good mental illness can ultimately produce then the stigma will be eventually reduced. It can result in greater faith, wider holiness, deeper love, and higher praise.

Mental illness can bring husbands and wives closer together. It can increase a pastor's sympathy and empathy. It can make a counselor useful. It can humble and sensitize sufferers. It can give insight into Christ's sufferings. It can open up ministry opportunities. Mental illnesses are not just problems but opportunities for growth, rapid growth, that those denied this experience are denied.

*God can turn the biggest negative
into a far greater positive.*

SUMMARY

Problem: Mental illness is stigmatized.

Insights: The stigma of mental illness is reduced by (1) education, (2) investment in lives, and (3) awareness of its positive results.

Action: Reduce stigma by education, involvement, and awareness of positive results.

- Regularly read books, both Christian and non-Christian, about mental illness.
- Listen to testimonies of sufferers with and survivors of mental illness.
- Meet with sufferers and ask for help to learn how to be helpful not harmful.
- Consider the kinds of positive results God can bring out of the most negative events.

Tom's Story about Cheryl

Before Cheryl decided to "go public" with her story of mental illness (schizoaffective disorder; story continued from chapter 15), many in church tended to avoid her. She was often disheveled and did not always remember to bathe regularly. Before returning to treatment and being stabilized on medications, she sometimes behaved rather strangely (later, folks learned that she was having much difficulty concentrating due to hearing voices in her head).

When she began to talk about her illness, people began to pay attention; she seemed easier to be around and to interact with. People seemed to realize that mental illness was not like a virus that they could catch but rather was like any other illness that needed care and compassion: Cheryl needed them, and they needed her. Everyone in church gradually learned that talking about mental illness:

- Makes it more understandable
- Allows others to develop empathy
- Informs of new opportunities to serve
- Gives permission for others to discuss struggles
- Reassures that mental illness is part of our broken human condition
- Encourages us to look forward to the day when God will wipe all tears from our eyes

29

How Can We Prepare
for Mental Illness?

LIKE MANY ILLNESSES, mental illness can strike someone out of the blue. We often hear people say, "That's the last person I thought would become depressed," or "What do they have to be anxious about?" or "It's not in their family." All of these responses suggest that people view mental illness as predictable. Sometimes it is, but not always. Otherwise, we could and would prepare for it. Instead, it usually finds us unprepared. We can't believe or accept that it's happening, often delaying our response to it. If we prepared, though, it could mean that it does not come; and, if it does, that we respond to it in more helpful ways.

We Can Prepare with Education

Although we will never know everything there is to know about any mental illness, we can get some basics in place. For example, we can learn about our own family history. Ask your parents and grandparents about whether there was any history of such illness in their lives or families. That way, we can discover if we might have a genetic tendency to it and take precautionary steps. By listening to our family's stories, we can hopefully learn whether we share some of the same characteristics of those who did suffer in this way.

Second, we can learn about the symptoms of different mental illnesses. We hope this book will give you an introduction to this, but we would encourage you to dig deeper and get more detail, so that you can spot it as early as possible. Perhaps read biographies and memoirs of those who have suffered in this way, but also you can check on websites online that give lists of symptoms to look out for.

Third, we can learn about the kind of habits and routines that are good (or bad) for mental health. That may involve changes in sleeping, eating, exercising, and working habits.

Education always takes time, but this kind of learning can save us a lot of time and pain in the long run. It can help prevent mental illness or mitigate and shorten it if it does strike. As the old saying goes, forewarned is forearmed.

Mental health education
limits mental illness experience.

That's fine for the mind. Can we make any spiritual preparations?

We Can Prepare with Scripture

One of the reasons we teach our children the Bible and Christian doctrine is so that they are equipped for whatever life throws at them. If our family history has a genetic tendency toward mental illness, then it would be wise to prepare our children for this by equipping them with specific verses and truths that prevent the onset of mental illness, that may protect them from its worst effects, or can preserve them in it. If we truly care for our children, we will build up their spiritual and biblical resources so that they have Scripture and truth readily available to call upon when they need it.

Ask yourself, what Scripture verses and truths would provide a firm foundation for our family members when the storms of depression or anxiety hit their shores? Why not memorize some of these verses together? Sing Scripture-saturated songs so that they are available to our loved ones in the darkness. Listen to sermons that deal with suffering, especially those that deal with mental and emotional suffering.

And, of course, we especially search the Scriptures to find Christ. Whether there is a genetic vulnerability or not, mental illness, including psychosis, can come upon anyone at any time, and therefore using our mental capacities while we *have* them to find and believe in Christ is an urgent matter and should not be delayed.

Fill your store with Scripture
for supply in times of suffering.

In what ways can the church prepare?

We Can Prepare the Church

One of the best ways we can prepare the church community for someone in the community having mental illness is to pray regularly for those with mental illness. That does not need to be by name, but can be simply a general prayer for the mentally ill. This normalizes mental illness and makes a big statement about its being okay to suffer in this way, that the church is concerned about it, and so is God.

Sermons may also help to prepare the church for dealing with mental illness, both the sufferers and the caregivers. Given how common it is, regular sermon applications can be directed toward the mentally ill, but also whole sermons and series of sermons could be preached. This too will help everyone to accept it when it comes and encourage people that the church is there to help them too.

Mental health support groups are also becoming increasingly common. These may meet every week or every month, with sufferers and caregivers together seeking to share their lives with one another and encourage one another. Just knowing that others are in the same position and are praying for them can be huge.

---

*A praying church
is a prepared church.*

SUMMARY

Problem: Mental illness often finds us unprepared.

Insights: We can prepare ourselves and our churches (1) with education, (2) with Scripture, and (3) with prayer.

Action: Prepare yourself, your family, and your church with education, Scripture, and prayer.

David's Story

As our children got into their teens, Shona and I began to share Shona's story with them. We gently and gradually introduced them to the concept of mental illness and how it had affected Shona. We did this partly to help them sympathize better with Shona's struggles but also to prepare them for what may be in their future due to their genetic inheritance. When, almost twenty years later, I experienced acute anxiety and realized I'd been suffering with chronic depression, we were totally open with our four older kids, while protecting our youngest (only six years old at the time). If there's a genetic component to my depression, and I believe there is, then our kids are up against it.

However, we tried to be positive about this by encouraging our children to be on the lookout for causes and symptoms of mental illness in themselves and their families, and also to take preventative measures that may spare them in the future. We look out for one another, and from time to time we check in with one another to make sure all is well and that we're taking all the steps we can to protect ourselves and our loved ones. We regularly pray for those with mental illness and never allow any mockery or demeaning of sufferers.

30

What Good Comes Out
of Mental Illness?

WHAT POSSIBLE GOOD can come out of mental illness? That's a question that sufferers and caregivers often ask amid the confusion and stress of caring for someone with mental illness. The answer is, there can be no good produced without God's blessing, but good can be multiplied *with* God's blessing (Rom. 8:28).

God is sovereign over mental illness, and he rules over it to produce good for those who love God, both sufferers and caregivers. He can take what seems like the worst garbage in our lives and turn it into something good and useful. Nothing is wasted in God's economy.

God's Blessing Produces Good Fruits in the Sufferer

Consider, first of all, the number and variety of fruits that God's blessing can produce in the sufferer.

God refocuses our attention. God uses depression to turn attention to him and away from the trivial and the artificial. Suffering redirects our minds and hearts and refocuses them on the God we neglected or took for granted when things were going well for us.

God renews the gospel. When sufferers can do nothing for God, not even offer a prayer, the gospel of grace, of salvation without our works, becomes more and more precious. The Christian sufferer can say, "God loves me and thinks of me even when I cannot love him or think of him." Amid so much that is bad and discouraging, the good news is so renewing and encouraging.

God reveals his strength. Although we may think that God's strength would be seen more clearly when we are strong, in reality God shows his strength far more clearly when we are weak. Then it's far more obvious that it's not ourselves but God who upholds us (2 Cor. 12:9–10).

God replaces ignorance with knowledge. Many who experience mental illness admit that, prior to their suffering, they never understood mental illness, or they misunderstood it. But through the experience, God has shown them their error and taught them what they didn't know.

God reemploys us in his service. Many who recover from mental illness go on to become counselors or caregivers or to serve the Lord in various other ways. They comfort others with the comfort with which they have been comforted (2 Cor. 1:3–7).

God revives his word. Parts of the Bible that were previously a mystery, especially the parts that deal with pain, suffering, and lament, open up with new beauty and power. Sufferers enter into the fellowship of Christ's sufferings in a new way (Phil. 3:10).

God restores joy. Although sufferers think they will never laugh or even smile again, when God does restore the joy of his salvation it is unforgettable and treasured as never before.

God reforms theology. We learn more about God through suffering than we ever can in seminary. We no longer see God as a harsh slavedriver but as a slave-emancipator. We no longer see him as driving us on with his whip, but as someone who loves to rest and refresh his people with his love.

God resensitizes us. We become more sensitive to physical, mental, emotional, spiritual, and relational changes and their impact on us and others.

God resurrects us. When God brings us out of mental illness, he gives us a foretaste of what the ultimate resurrection will be like. It's a mini-resurrection, a little sample or appetizer of the great final resurrection.

God redirects us. Whereas before we didn't think much of heaven, but rather were taken up with this world, mental illness gives us a new longing for heaven, where all pain, sadness, and fear will be removed and we will be given perfect physical, emotional, mental, spiritual, and relational health.

God's blessing can transform
rotten fruit into ripe fruit.

What about the caregivers? Any good for them in all this?

God's Blessing Produces Good Fruits in the Caregivers

Many of the good fruits in the lives of sufferers are duplicated in the lives of the caregivers. Families, friends, and church communities may see many of these same fruits in their own lives as a result of caring for those with mental illness. But there are additional fruits they should expect and cultivate.

We learn dependence. Caring for the mentally ill teaches us to become less self-dependent and more dependent on God. Our needs are far greater than what we can supply, and therefore we turn to God to fully supply them (Phil. 4:19).

We learn to pray. Formal and shallow prayer is left behind and replaced with real and desperate prayer. Prayer becomes passionate and permanent, not sleepy and sporadic.

We learn compassion. Impatience with and disinterest in the weakness of others is replaced with kind and thoughtful care.

We learn service. We begin to live a life devoted to the good of others, even if it involves sacrificing our own comfort and desires. This servant-heart then carries over into other areas of life as well.

We learn to counsel. We discover so many of God's therapeutic resources in his word and world, and we grow in the skillful use of both to provide hope, help, and healing.

We learn patience. There's no other way to grow the patience muscle than through trial and affliction. Suffering pumps up our puny patience muscle.

We learn prevention. Most Christians prevent physical illness by using various strategies but rarely do the same when it comes to mental illness. Caring for sufferers changes that because we realize how much we need to take preemptive steps to avoid falling into the same trap.

We learn sensitivity. Whereas before, we would not have spotted mental illness in others, we now have sensitized antennae and we're able to detect it and offer care and assistance. We're also able to see its early beginnings in ourselves and take the appropriate precautionary steps.

We learn the value of church. We see how much we need to hear the word, worship God, be prayed for, and enjoy community. Though caregivers, we also need care, and the church can provide that support.

We learn about Christ. As we learn these lessons and bear these fruits in our lives, we come to realize how Jesus learned these lessons in his own humanity and bore these same fruits even as he went through the darkest and most terrifying experiences.

None of this education happens automatically. Like all affliction in the lives of Christians, mental illness is a talent that has to be used the right way to bring a return on investment that does good to us and brings glory to God (Matt. 25:14–30). Even non-Christians realize this. For example, the authors of *Mind over Mood* illustrate it this way:

> An oyster creates a pearl out of a grain of sand. The grain of sand is an irritant to the oyster. In response to the discomfort, the oyster creates a smooth, protective coating that encases the sand and provides relief. The result is a beautiful pearl. For an oyster, an irritant becomes the seed for something new.[1]

Let's take this sand, and with God's help turn it into great good for us and others, and great glory to God.

---

*A grain of irritating sand
can graduate as a beautiful pearl.*

SUMMARY

Problem: Mental illness seems pointless and profitless.

1   Dennis Greenberger and Christine Padesky, *Mind over Mood* (New York: Guilford, 1995), 1.

Insights: God's blessing produces (1) good fruits in the sufferer and (2) good fruits in the caregiver.

Action: By grace, invest the talent of mental illness so that it produces a great spiritual return for our good and God's glory.

Tom's Story

The following verses have provided me with much instruction and comfort, both in my own struggle and in my assisting others in their struggles.

God promises in 1 Peter 5:10, "And after you have suffered a little while, the God of all grace, who has called you to his eternal glory in Christ, will himself restore, confirm, strengthen, and establish you." Our struggles do not escape God's watchful and compassionate eye. He is working through our struggles for our good and his glory.

In Ephesians 4, Paul describes how God has equipped each of his children for a special purpose in his kingdom, for service in the local church. In verse 16 he writes, "from whom the whole body, joined and held together by every joint with which it is equipped, when each part is working properly, makes the body grow so that it builds itself up in love." In God's loving care, we have been placed in our local church both to serve and to be served by brothers and sisters in Christ, for their sanctification and for ours.

The Story behind This Book

When Norman Van Mersbergen's brother, Gary, died from complications of schizophrenia, a small legacy of about $70,000 was realized from his estate. Due to their painful experience of trying to care for Gary through these traumatic years, Norman and his wife, Vicki, felt called of God to donate this money to a research project that would ultimately help Christians care for other Christians with mental illness.

They reached out to Dr. David Murray, then a professor of counseling, and along with Ed Stetzer they pulled together a team from Lifeway and Focus on the Family to research this neglected subject. The resulting research is the foundation of this book. Here is a little of Norman's (and Vicki's) story.

Norman's Story

My wife, sister, and I were sitting in a small hospital waiting room on Christmas Eve. It was not a "joy-to-the-world" moment. My brother was in surgery to have part of his lung removed. The doctors had diagnosed lung cancer in August, and, after some postponements for medical reasons, surgery was finally scheduled for December 24.

My brother was a ward of the state. He was 50, divorced, had no children, and had not been gainfully employed for 20 years. The medical team exemplified a host of people who had over the years given tender compassion and practical aid to my brother. His need was constant and great because Gary was mentally ill. The terms rather run together now: words like bipolar, manic depressive, schizophrenic, schizoid-affect, psychotic. One word stands out and stood out: voices.

Some thirty-three years ago, in the spring, my brother was tilling the soil ahead of my father, who was doing the planting. Strangely, Gary stopped his tractor in the middle of the field, walked over to our dad, and announced that he wanted to make a profession of faith right away and was leaving the field to go visit with the minister. I was in basic training at the time, when Mom wrote to tell me that Gary was going to make a profession of faith and become a communicant member of the church.

That is the first incident which, looking back, suggested the onset of mental illness. What happened from there is now a blur in my mind because of the years of drama and trauma. Gary married and moved out of state, but two years later he and his wife moved back to begin their farming career. They never produced a crop. By that time, he was on medication and had been hospitalized once. He simply could not cope with the pressure of making decisions for the business. Their marriage lasted four years.

His illness was getting worse. One day, my wife was hanging clothes on the clothesline, when he spun his pickup dangerously around her on the lawn. Weeks later, I had to go get his pickup out of the ditch after he rolled it. Sometime following that, he was admitted to a mental hospital. Medication helped a little, as did shock treatments. He drove out of state and wrecked his pickup near a school. Then the drinking started, resulting in the loss of his license and insurance. One day, the police found him standing naked on the highway in the winter. More hospitalization. He ended up in two different group homes, and there I would visit and take him out for lunch. He asked me to take him to the supermarket, where he bought a grocery bag of coffee. He would take it to his room to get a caffeine high against the institution's rules. At the second group home, he would walk to town and visit with the farmers in the café.

Gary lived three hours away from us, but was friends with an elderly couple. He attended a local church, even though he was mostly critical of the minister. During this time, he stayed on medication better than in his earlier years. In fact, he became an expert on medication and would advise the doctor on what he should have. He also knew the side-effects of each medication.

So, there we are in the waiting room of the hospital on Christmas Eve, three decades after the signs of the onset of mental illness. The lung cancer was serious, and we had several good conversations with him about quitting smoking. We decided to wash all his clothes, bedding, and so forth, and contacted a cleaning service to clean the apartment as the nicotine stain from smoke was everywhere. Gary had committed to trying to quit, and we knew a clean home would help him in that.

During one of our visits after his surgery, Gary wanted us to bring his pickup to the hospital. I assumed he wanted it there once he was discharged. As requested, we put his pickup in the parking lot. On this day he was awake and doing quite well physically, but little did I know that this would be our last conversation with him. It was a rather one-sided conversation: "Where are my shoes?" "In your pickup." "Why didn't you bring them up?" "I didn't know you wanted them." I do not remember much after that. We never saw him again. He didn't want us around. He died alone, two years later, of an aneurysm.

This is our story of the decades of turmoil we all experienced. It is important to have a context when discussing such serious issues and asking the hard questions that they provoke. Gary was our context, and you have your own. This is part of a long process of trying to look at one life of mental illness in the context of these words: "But the fruit of the Spirit is love, joy, peace, longsuffering, kindness, goodness, faithfulness, gentleness, self-control" (Gal. 5:22–23). Gary professed faith, but what fruits of faith were in his life? What fruits of faith are possible in such a life? What do the fruits of faith look like in a life like this? How do we discern the fruit of faith in a life that looks as if it's ruled by the works of the flesh?

Recently, my wife was having a conversation with a woman she did not know. The lady asked my wife her name. Upon hearing her name, the lady's face blanched and she said that years ago my brother had tried to burn down their apartment, which he was renting. After all these years, if one were to ask this lady in which category my brother fit, the category of Galatians 5:19–21 (works of the flesh) or Galatians 5:22–26 (fruits of the Spirit), my wife is sure that her reaction would indicate the former. This lady was a member of the church where my brother and parents had been members.

After his death, I received many of my brother's personal items. Slowly, as time and courage would permit, I started to look at them. Eventually I found a letter in which he addressed God as "Dear Father in Heaven," asking him to relieve the mental pressure and help him to stop looking over his shoulder.

I know he would never have shared this with me. It was only after his death, fourteen years after he wrote this entry, that I had my first glimpse of a spark of Galatians 5:22–24 in my brother. It is only a glimpse, but I now know that others saw glimpses as well. Those glimpses didn't put a particular statement or action of his in the context of the fruit of the Spirit, but that doesn't matter. What matters is that on December 27, 1998, Gary addressed Almighty God as "Dear Father in Heaven." Had I known this before, I might have used this glimpse of faith to redirect many conversations, such as the one we had in the hospital. What is clear to me now is that this "dear Father in heaven" moment suggests an awareness of the redemptive work of Christ on behalf of my brother, and that in spite of his broken brain, Gary verbalized it.

In the providence of God, albeit a dark one, my brother's brain was broken and mangled by mental illness. In his grace, God allowed that brain to yet work in such a way as to come to faith. However, Gary's brain was still broken and for 35 years that brain was capable of manufacturing voices; that brain could become delusional; that brain was bipolar; and that brain could be terribly destructive. Yet there was a glimpse—a glimpse of spiritual fruit.

The purpose of this book is to help the reader understand how the broken brain does not work, to set the broken brain in the context of the gospel, and to discover how the church can bring comfort to the mentally ill and their families by watching for a Galatians 5:22–24 moment.

Norman Van Mersbergen
December, 2020

General Index

abnormal, 23, 31, 32, 33, 36
"abnormal abnormality," 31
About Mental Illness (NAMI report), 16n1
Acute Mental Illness and Christian Faith. See *Study of Acute Mental Illness and Christian Faith* (Lifeway Research report)
Adam and Eve, 82
affective (mood) disorders, 24, 27, 39, 40
antianxiety drugs, 133
antidepressants, 133, 134, 186
anxiety, 1, 1n1, 2, 3, 4, 8, 20, 24, 25, 26, 31, 36, 49, 52, 53, 60, 68, 73, 76, 82, 87, 92, 100, 102, 103, 105, 111, 124, 132, 133, 145, 164, 199, 216, 223, 225; abnormal anxiety, 36; normal anxiety, 31; social anxiety disorder, 24
assumptions, false, 95

Baxter, Richard, 9n2
biblical counselors, 139–44
bipolar disorder (manic depression), 1, 8, 20, 24, 26–27, 82, 89, 125, 234, 238
boundaries, 117, 211, 212, 213
Burns, David D., 41n1

"Can Depression Be Cured? Recent Research" (Murray article), 43, 50, 134
caregivers, 5, 100, 103, 128, 129, 146, 148, 156, 174, 209–14, 224, 227, 228, 229, 230, 232; *see also* mental illness: caregivers and
Chandra, Anjali, 91
Cheryl, Tom's story about, 113, 120–21, 129–30, 219
church/church family, 1, 2, 3, 4n3, 5, 8, 8n1, 9, 13, 30, 43, 55, 56, 58, 62, 80, 87, 89, 97n2, 98, 102, 103, 105, 107–13, 107n1, 108n2, 108n4, 109n5, 111n6, 117, 118, 120, 123, 128, 130, 139, 140, 141, 142, 145, 146, 147, 148, 154n8, 155n9, 167–72, 173, 180, 181, 185–86, 194, 197, 204, 210, 211, 215, 219, 223–24, 229, 230, 232, 234, 235, 237, 238
clinical depression. *See* major depressive disorder (clinical depression)
comfort, false, 47
confusion, 7, 12, 13, 23, 29, 31, 47, 48, 55, 56, 57, 59, 62, 81, 132, 140, 201, 227
counseling/counselors, 18, 54, 96, 97, 101, 102, 103, 104, 132, 135, 139–43, 230

personality disorders, 8
phobia, specific, 25
physical depression, 9; *see also* depression; sadness; spiritual depression
post-partum depression, 26; *see also* depression
Preservatives against Melancholy and Over-Much Sorrow (Baxter book), 9n2
primary care physician (PCP), 124, 127, 129
promises, false, 188
psychosis. *See* mind (thought) disorders: psychosis
post-traumatic stress disorder (PTSD), 25; *see also* anxiety
Puritans, 9, 83
"Puritans and Mental Illness, The" (Murray article), 83n3; *see also* Puritans

rationalization, 66, 69; *see also* mental illness: reactions to
reactive (situational) depression, 26; *see also* depression
relationships. *See* church/church family; family; friends/friendships; mental illness: family/friends and
Reset: Living a Grace-Paced Life in a Burnout Culture (Murray book), 4n4, 49n4

sadness, 16, 26, 31–37, 40, 56, 132, 140, 229; abnormal sadness, 31–33, 36; normal sadness, 33, 36; *see also* depression; physical depression; spiritual depression
Sally, Tom's story about, 37
schizophrenia. *See* mind (thought) disorders: schizophrenia
Scott, Tom's story about, 30, 62–63

Serving Those with Mental Illness (Focus on the Family resource), 4n3, 103n11, 108n3, 159n2, 211n1; *see also* Focus on the Family
"shoulds," false, 188
social anxiety disorder. *See* anxiety: social anxiety disorder
spiritual depression, 9n2; *see also* depression; physical depression; sadness
spiritual growth. *See* mental illness: spiritual growth and
spirituality, false, 134
stigma. *See* mental illness: stigma of
Study of Acute Mental Illness and Christian Faith (Lifeway Research report), 4n3, 8n1, 9n3, 24n1, 27n5, 47nn1–2, 48n3, 50nn6–8, 52n9, 56n1, 97nn1–2, 98nn3–4, 99n5, 101n7, 103nn9–10, 107n1, 108n2, 108n4, 109n5, 111n6, 117n1, 123n1, 124n2, 131n1, 133n2, 135n4, 151nn1–3, 152n4, 153nn5–7, 154n8, 155n9, 159n1, 159n2; *see also* faith/faithfulness; Lifeway Research; mental illness: faith and
suicide, 201–7
support team, 116, 117, 119, 120; *see also* church/church family; friends/friendships; mental illness: family/friends and

temptation. *See* mental illness: temptation and
thinking, false, 84
transformation, false, 41

Van Mersbergen, Gary, 3, 4, 233–38
Van Mersbergen, Norman, 3, 233, 238
Van Mersbergen, Vicki, 3

Scripture Index

More Resources
from David Murray

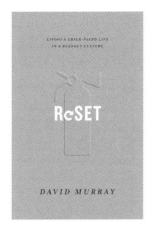

For more information, visit **crossway.org**.